SCOTS IN UNIFORM

Published 1972 by Holmes McDougall Ltd.
30 Royal Terrace, Edinburgh EH7 5AL.

© Douglas N. Anderson

ISBN 7157 1254-3

Printed by Holmes McDougall Ltd., Tay Street, Perth.

SCOTS IN UNIFORM
The Military Costume of Scotland's Horse and Foot
by Douglas N. Anderson

To
Elizabeth and Virginia
who help and encourage.

Contents

Introduction	6
Preface	10
Foreword	11
8/9 Bn The Royal Scots (The Royal Regiment) (TA)	13
4/5 Bn Royal Scots Fusiliers (TA)	17
4/5th Bn The King's Own Scottish Borderers (TA)	21
6/7th Bn The Cameronians (Scottish Rifles) (TA)	25
6/7th Bn The Black Watch (TA)	29
5/6th Bn The Highland Light Infantry (TA)	33
11th Bn Seaforth Highlanders (TA)	37
3rd Bn The Gordon Highlanders (TA)	41
4/5th Bn The Queen's Own Cameron Highlanders (TA)	45
7th & 8th Bns The Argyll & Sutherland Highlanders (TA)	49
1st Scots Troop of Life Guards	53
2nd Scots Troop Horse Grenadiers	57
East Lothian Yeomanry Cavalry	61
The Scots Greys	65
The Lanarkshire Yeomanry	69
Fife Light Horse Volunteers	73
Artillery Volunteers	77
Highland Company of Mounted Infantry	81
The Ayrshire Yeomanry Cavalry	85
Queen's Own Royal Glasgow Yeomanry	89
Scottish Horse Imperial Yeomanry	93
The Lovat Scouts	97
Appendix	101

Introduction

FROM India to Indiana the popular image of the Scottish soldier is of the kilt, bonnet and bagpipes. There are many, and good reasons why this should be. But the tartan, however conspicuous, is only a part in the evolution of Scottish military costume, and from a span of several hundred years it is obvious that the full narrative is long and complex. Anyone who has had contact with the subject, however marginal, will know just how complex; those who come to it here relatively innocent will find, not a chronological history but rather some connected episodes.

Primarily this is a picture book of soldiers. The words are there to provide background and comment to the plates, dates occur only where necessary or to establish context so that a historical sequence is, in fact, present.

Military uniforms are open history books; they may be looked at and enjoyed without understanding, or, if you know the language they may be read *and* enjoyed. Given the country of origin, any one uniform is subject to five conditions: regiment, date, rank, order of dress, and geographical situation. Before he puts pencil to paper the military artist must have satisfactory answers to each of these. Research provides the answers and the veracity of the finished work stands or falls by the sources of reference. The obstacles on the path to accuracy are formidable. Curiously, the difficulties of historical research are not really in proportion to distance in time. The Second World War ended not so long ago but already film-makers are getting even the most elementary things wrong – the greater the volume of reference, the wider the scope for error.

Printed and pictorial records, original contemporary articles and, occasionally, verbatim reports, all provide sources and must all be treated with equal caution. Published regulations tend to be vague and to avoid descriptions of the unorthodox (notably Scottish) items with an evasive, "of regimental pattern". In any case, many regulations merely gave official approval to customs which had been practised for years; for example, the bayonet belt was authorised to be moved from the waist to the right shoulder in 1784 because so many regiments were wearing it that way already – for the same reason it was ordered back to the waist again in 1852.

Also, the date on which new patterns of clothing were ordered is no indication of how long the change would take to reach regiments serving abroad.

Pictorial reference prior to the camera may be just as bewildering. Dated portraits were often painted to celebrate days of former glory and show the sitter wearing an obsolete uniform in a fanciful setting. Artists, it must be

Six

admitted, could be woefully inaccurate either through ignorance or for commercial considerations — after all, the cavalry charge is only half as splendid when plumes have been removed, headdresses covered by foul-weather covers and horses and men stripped of decoration. Of these two misleading sins ignorance is the worse.

Sometimes areas of ignorance are inevitable where complete information simply doesn't exist and gaps have to be filled by reasoned guesswork. In this book a very few of the earlier uniforms required a little reconstruction and this is acknowledged in the texts.

In the late 1840's a new flow of information is quite suddenly available in photography. Now the uniforms and equipment can be seen without the distortion of human error. Unfortunately, this particular bogey, far from being eliminated, shifts from the artist to the sitter. Illuminating as it is in regard to details of dress, weapons and custom, and for this the camera is of immeasureable value, the ultimate worth of each print lies in its being a frozen moment of a precise time. Ungrateful as it may sound, the interpretation of this set against previous knowledge may be baffling in the extreme. (Why does that piper wear no dirk? Was it a short-lived regimental whim, or did he fall into his clothes the morning after and forget to put it on?) Studio portraits are notably misleading with sitters improving their uniforms for the occasion the better to impress.

The British soldier is incorrigible in the "improvement" of his clothes wherever and whenever he can get away with it. In the late 1940's many a "best BD" blouse was unpicked, reassembled and pressed in imitation of the US Army combat jacket. On campaign the soldier is quick to adapt, in past eras justifiably so, for in times of peace uniforms invariably became more elaborate and restricting. The Light Cavalry regiments embarking for the Crimea wore gorgeous clothes so close-fitting that the men could only mount with care and make no other strenuous movements — yet they were off to fight a war!

In the field, officers were inclined to dress and equip themselves after the manner of the sporting clothes of country gentlemen. The Rank and File were supposed to put up with regulation issues, and if left to fend for themselves soon conveniently lost or cut up anything which was too tight or too heavy.

Early campaigns are usually poorly documented pictorially. Home-based artist-reporters, working from superficial knowledge, for an uncritical public, frequently perpetrated wild inaccuracies under "artistic licence". Letters and accounts are tantalisingly vague — understandably. For the 74th Highlander in the Kaffir War it was enough to mention that he exchanged his red coat for the canvas blouse which had been issued while at sea; it would never occur to him to describe this garment in detail, nor to keep a specimen of the locally made wooden water-kegs carried by each man. How many Regimental Museums are storing the paraphernalia of to-day for the benefit of tomorrow's student?

Regrettably the amount of early equipment which survives is very small; much of it was used until it wore out. Similarly with clothing; although fine officers' uniforms, carefully preserved after service, are plentiful by comparison with contemporary Rank and File items. The majority of these would be worn until they disintegrated. Until the wearing of the Queen's uniform other than by serving soldiers was forbidden by law in 1894 there was nothing to prevent its use by anybody. Old soldiers had been allowed to wear their regimentals after discharge and the abuse of uniforms by advertising sandwich men had become a public scandal. Up to that date, therefore, wear and tear would account for vast numbers of humble, but none the less interesting, uniforms.

In fact, most uniforms started off as comparatively plain utility garments with small differentiations of rank and regiment. After the establishment of the first Standing Army in 1660 soldiers were clothed in a modification of civilian dress with necessary arms and equipment hung about them. At this time Scottish regiments looked no different from any others in the land. The first Highland regiment, and therefore the first tartan, appeared with the raising of the Black Watch in 1739. A great many other Highland corps followed before the end of the century, all of them clad in tartan. The older Lowland regiments, however, were still dressed and armed like the rest of the Line.

Undoubtedly the survival of Highland dress after the Proscription Act owed much to these early Highland regiments. The Act took effect in 1747 and remained in force until 1782 – a mere 35 years, but time enough seriously to damage the natural evolution of the national costume, so vigorously was it applied. Only in the army was tartan condoned and after the repeal of the Act its revival was limited and, at first, largely influenced by this one remaining channel to the past. Although it could not possibly have been evident at the time this was the opening which would admit changes to Scottish military dress and eventually direct the course of our national costume.

The "celtic revival" of the mid-1800's was clearly stimulated by the visit to Edinburgh in 1822 by George IV and later the affection of Queen Victoria for things Scottish; but neither alone would have been significant without the public enthusiasm for tartan which ran riot over clothes, furnishing fabrics, ornaments and souvenirs. In complete contradiction to the previous century civilian Highland dress now borrowed extensively and openly from the military but exaggerating and embellishing it until by late Victorian times it was such a vulgar travesty that one marvels at its survival at all.

At the Army Reforms of 1881 the Lowland regiments were put into a semi-Highland dress, thereby setting a curious style which is now nearly a century old.

The effects of the reforms went very much farther than changes in dress, and one which was felt deeply saw an end to the old system of regimental numbers. After 1660, as new regiments had been formed, they were known by the name of a person connected with their raising or command such as "Lord Leven's" or "The Earl of Mar's" (later KOSB and RSF respectively). This pleasant custom persisted well into the next century; at the same time, however, a system of numbering had been introduced in 1694. It was supposedly based upon seniority and its extension should have simplified the sequence of British Line regiments unequivocally. In practice the creation of new corps following the disbandment of old ones, the reallocation of numbers and addition of others produced a fine confusion which makes parts of regimental histories read more like algebra than English. For instance, the 43rd (The Black Watch) were renumbered the 42nd, the 73rd became the 71st, the 78th changed to the 72nd (later 1st Seaforth) while the new 78th eventually became 2nd Seaforth – and this ignores earlier regiments who may have held the same numbers previously.

This was the situation up to 1881 when the entire organisation of the Army was examined from War Office to sentry-box.

The changes which affected the regimental system were radical and far reaching. Edward Cardwell, as Secretary of State for War, assisted by Garnet Wolseley, devised a scheme whereby two regiments were to be linked to form one regiment of two battalions, one battalion to remain at home supplying trained men to the other overseas. Instead of bearing the old, and by now historic, numbers, the new regiments were to be given names relating to the territorial recruiting areas allotted to them and were to be designated as 1st and 2nd Battalion accordingly. The system applied only to regiments of one battalion and therefore did not affect those numbered up to 25. Needless to say some of the unions were rather uneasy and the standardisation of dress for both battalions often provoked discord (which was sometimes sustained by old die-hards right up until their retirement). As far as the general public was concerned the greatest impact came from the emergence of names which were to be common currency for years to come, names familiar to all Scotland until the Army reductions in the 1950's.

Meanwhile throughout the century, in a series of national crises, literally hundreds of thousands of men had offered themselves in immense volunteer armies. The enthusiasm of these part-time auxiliaries was limited only by Government economy although a few, notably some Yeomanry corps, managed to maintain unbroken service. In an Act of 1907 the Volunteers and Yeomanry were transferred to a new Territorial Force as an appendage of the Regular Army, many adapting, in part or whole, the uniform of the Regular regiment to whose territorial area they were assigned. But the strength which grew from this association was not to be fully appreciated until 1914.

Subject to international and political climate the historical pattern of alternate reduction and expansion of the Armed Forces continues even to-day. Public sympathy is currently cool towards the military and largely indifferent to the Volunteer. Yet in this dangerously technological age there is still a place for men with old-fashioned concepts of duty.

In Scotland there is a military tradition of bravery and loyal service. From ancient times the poverty of the country, the hard nature of life and a fierce natural pride bred a fighting man of rare independence. In due course these qualities and pride encompassed his entire regiment, its Colours and emblems, generating a potent "family" feeling and a unique character. These were deep roots which struggled to defy pruning and in spite of standardisation old names, tartans and devices survive. Through them the past keeps a toe-hold on the present, embodied in the uniforms and individual distinctions of custom and dress of the Scottish regiments.

In 1599 a foreign monarch wrote in praise and honour of the Scottish Men-at-Arms who, incredibly, by their achievements had risen to become his premier troops and Bodyguard.

Might not his elegant accolade have been written of any and all Scottish soldiers?

".....the graces and privileges whereof they have rendered themselves worthy, through the affection and fidelity which they have borne this crown." *Henry IV., King of France.*

Preface

THE water-colour paintings which are reproduced in this book first appeared in the pages of Scottish Field magazine, in two separate series, divided by a number of years but both under the heading of SCOTS IN UNIFORM.

The first, the series of Scottish Territorial Army regiments, was featured in five monthly issues during 1966 and was inspired by the impending reorganisation of the Reserve Forces in which it was anticipated there would be reductions and perhaps even the complete disappearance of some old and valued corps. Where this would have had particular significance was in those TA battalions who alone still bore the names of famous parent regiments already sacrificed to Government pruning. The subjects for illustration were all chosen from the TA battalions of the ten Scottish Infantry regiments which existed before the Regular Army amalgamations of 1959.

The reorganisation of the Reserve took effect on April 1, 1967. The establishment for Scotland provided for two composite battalions, one Highland and one Lowland, and a number of Territorial battalions, there being two classifications, T & AVR II and AVR III. In practical terms what this might mean was that a regiment previously of battalion establishment was now reduced to company status within the new battalion framework; thus the 8/9th Bn. The Royal Scots (TA) became 'A' company, The 52nd Lowland Volunteers (T & AVR II). Each Volunteer company was permitted to retain the uniform and insignia of its predecessor, thereby maintaining cherished individualities and honours. Subsequently, the structure was expanded and 2nd Battalions with separate Headquarters were added to each of the Highland and Lowland Volunteers. Cadres of officers and NCO's who had been specially earmarked for the role formed the basis of the new 'regimental' companies.

The series of paintings, therefore, was intended to show some of the more colourful uniforms worn by the Scottish Infantry regiments of the Territorial Army in 1966, some of which it was suspected might vanish. The accompanying texts made no effort to be potted unit histories, this information being available elsewhere; instead, an attempt was made to describe some of the traditional and regimental distinctions of dress and custom. For this book these texts have been almost entirely rewritten to more than twice the original length and references to current situations which were relevant in 1966 have now been omitted.

The second Scottish Field series showing Scottish mounted regiments was featured over 12 issues from July, 1971 to June, 1972 and began with The Royal Scots Greys, chosen deliberately to coincide with their amalgamation with the 3rd Carabiniers. The aim thereafter was to illustrate and describe only a few of the very many regiments of cavalry, Regular and Auxiliary, which have existed in Scotland at various times over the past three hundred or so years. Some of these had a relatively brief life span; others, grown older and drastically altered, are still with us. The articles which accompanied these pictures are reprinted here almost unchanged, but now in chronological order.

Finally, the ultimate destinies of all of the subjects at the time of writing are shown in an Appendix at the end of the book.

SCOTS IN UNIFORM

Foreword by Major-General R.E. Urquhart, C.B., D.S.O.

APART from the magnificent spectacle of the annual Trooping the Colour on the Horse Guards Parade in London, and the occasional guard of honour for a visiting important person, the general public sees little of the soldier in full dress uniform. The present day picture of the soldier shows him in a form of battle dress in which he may be emerging from some kind of armoured carrier in Germany; jungle-bashing in Malaya; or, and more likely, wearing a steel helmet with a visor and carrying a shield to ward off the assaults of stone throwing youths in Northern Ireland. But these soldiers, too, can lay on a ceremonial parade, with impeccable drill, and can wear dress with emblems and marks of difference of which they are immensely and justly proud. It may be that these outward signs of distinction had their origins in an event which took place several hundred years ago; they may have been acquired in battle, or possibly they are retained and worn as a reminder of parent regiments, which over a long period of years have suffered amalgamations or disbandments.

Military millinery has always attracted interest. But only those who have been concerned with a change of dress, or have served in a unit in which some alteration has been forced on it without the wish of those affected, can appreciate the heat engendered and the feelings that are aroused, which can be out of all proportion to the importance of the occasion. But, in this, some hint is given of the strength of that the most valuable factor — the pride in regiment — which contributes so much to the morale of any unit, whatever its role, and irrespective of the arm of the service to which it belongs. Distinctions in dress, however small, encourage a pride in belonging to a body in which there is mutual respect among all ranks. Rivalry in smartness of turnout between units is healthy and contributes much to this esprit de corps.

Uniformity in military dress has taken centuries to evolve. It was found to be a valuable aid to discipline. A smart uniform helped to develop self-confidence in the soldier and attracted recruits. In ancient times it also impressed the enemy!

The knights in medaevial times wore personal symbols on their armour. Heraldic devices appeared on their shields, surcoats and flags. While the leaders had these devices to show who they were, their followers wore badges or scarves, or things in their hats, such as feathers or plumes. It was not until the 17th century, during the Civil War, that the "red coat" appeared in the English armies, and more definite efforts made to regularise the clothes of the opposing sides in battle.

It is well over 300 years since Montrose, when in command of the Royalist army, and on his way to do battle with the Covenanters, outside Aberdeen in 1644, "bade his men plunder the adjacent cornfields and, in order to distinguish themselves from the enemy, stick each a bunch of oats in his bonnet." A blue ribbon was the mark of the Covenanter. And, some months later, at the battle of Kilsyth, the infantry in Montrose's army, partly because of the heat of the day, but mainly in order to prevent any lack of identity when the moment of hand-to-hand conflict was reached, were ordered to be prepared to fight in their shirts of coarse saffron, with the tails knotted between their legs. And the Royalist horsemen wore their shirts above their buff jerkins for the same purpose.

Commissions were issued by both sides in the Civil War to private gentlemen to raise regiments, and to clothe and equip the men who joined. This privilege lent great scope for individual taste in the adornments which were added. The larger the purse, the more elaborate the end result. In Scotland, hodden grey was introduced as the colour of the coat for the infantry. But officers of this arm, and all ranks in the cavalry, wore more colourful clothes. In later times, the red coat was worn by many Scottish regiments, but now this colour is only used by the Scots Guards and by infantry officers in their mess dress, the short jacket of the mess kit being the descendant of an unbuttoned red coat.

The first real breakaway from the traditional military dress came with the wars in South Africa. Khaki was introduced as a colour for the field dress, and sharp lessons from that natural soldier, the Boer, brought many changes in the weapons and equipment of the British Army. The use of mounted infantry was introduced, and several Scottish companies were among these units, the other ranks of whom wore puttees, which had been inspired by the Indian Army, and were at first made up from long strips of torn blankets. The Scottish Yeomanry regiments first saw action in South Africa.

Typical of this campaign is the Scottish Horse, now a unit of the R.C.T. They served as Medium gunners in the last war, but they owed their origin to the Caledonian Society of Johannesburg, who raised a mounted corps of South African Scots to fight in the Boer War. The Lanarkshire Yeomanry were raised to deal with riots in their county area; and an idea at a dinner party of members of the local hunt was the source of the Fife Light Horse Volunteers, forerunner of the Fife and Forfar Yeomanry, which later was to become a battalion of the Black Watch.

The Regular Army tended to set the fashion in dress which generally was reproduced in the regiments of volunteers. There was great enthusiasm for the volunteer forces in the 1800's and the Commanding Officers of newly raised units added much to the basic official uniform in the way of coloured facings and gold lace. These volunteers were the forerunners of the Territorial Army which contributed so much in the 1914 war. Even if they were short of training, the spirit which existed in these units was to prove invaluable when they took the field. The London Scottish and the Glasgow Highlanders were among the first T.A. battalions in action, and were fighting in France in November, 1914. They were closely followed by the 51st (Highland) Division. There was a similar pattern demonstrating the volunteer effort in 1939. It is sad to see this great asset — the military use of the voluntary spirit — given such a meagre chance of showing itself today, particularly when the reserves for the Regular Army are practically non-existant.

There is a deal of fascination in this study of military uniforms and the background of the regiments which wore them. There have been many books on the subject, but few authors are as accurate as Douglas Anderson in the detail of the dress of the regiments and corps which he has described. He is a specialist in this subject, and is particularly knowledgeable on the dress worn by units raised in Scotland over the centuries. In this work he has reminded us of a way of life and of uniforms which are gone for ever. It is, therefore, all the better for their recording.

The Scottish Regiments have contributed much to the history of Scotland.

8/9th. Bn. THE ROYAL SCOTS (THE ROYAL REGIMENT) (TA)

'FIRST OF FOOT, Right of the Line and Pride of the British Army' is an old if rather jingoistic definition of The Royal Scots based, in part anyway, on its position of seniority over all other Infantry of the Line. Actually, when Charles I and the Privy Council of Scotland gave warrant for Sir John Hepburn of Athelstaneford to recruit for his Scots regiment in the service of the French they were only giving Royal and official sanction to a body of fighting men which could trace its origins in the bands of Scots irregulars of two centuries earlier. Although Hepburn's soldiers fought on foreign soil it is this Royal authority of 1633 which establishes the undeniable seniority of the regiment in the service of the British Crown.

A second battalion was authorised in 1686 and from that date the regiment held the unique record of never being fewer than of two-battalion strength, that is until the Army reductions of 1949. This was to be a matter of consequence in 1881 because it meant that The Royal Scots was unaffected then by Cardwell's Reform system of linking pairs of one-battalion regiments.

But the reforms did bring changes and not too welcome ones at that. For two-and-a-half centuries the Royal Scots had served as a Regiment of Line and had been dressed as such in the normal pattern of clothing. The "Englishness" of this had been largely unremarked since it was not a Highland corps, and besides, nationalism had been privately expressed in the dress of the pipers which the regiment had maintained for many of its earlier years. After 1881, however, those Scottish regiments which were not

Highland found themselves clearly designated as "Lowland Scottish" and clothed in what they justifiably considered a kind of quasi-Highland fancy dress. The plain Line tunic was replaced by the skirted Highland doublet of 1856 pattern, and the dark trousers by ones of Government tartan. At this point official invention seems to have dried up and the existing full dress headdress, the spiked blue Home Pattern helmet, was rather incongruously retained. The undress cap at least had Scottish origins, being the glengarry bonnet to which dicing had been added in 1880. Officers were given a Highland sash and basket-hilted broadsword and adopted a badge taken from the Thistle Star of the 3rd Edinburgh Militia Battalion.

At first this costume was much resented by those compelled to wear it but to the average Scotsman, however, the picture was probably less bizarre. By this time the tartan mystique, started earlier in the century and encouraged by the Queen, was in full swing and all manner of eccentricities were being perpetrated in the name of tradition. Accustomed to some pretty extravagant Volunteer uniforms there would be little of note in a Line helmet topping a tunic, which was itself a piece of pure invention, over tartan trousers which owed nothing to historic costume except the pattern. Widely and incorrectly termed "trews" these garments bore little resemblance to the skin-tight trunk hose of the Highland gentleman worn for riding and travelling in past times. These had been skillfully cut with the tartan on the cross and seamed so as properly to display the small sett. At least one great Highland commandant believed the trews to be the most ancient form of Highland dress and clothed his regiment accordingly. The splendid, often-reproduced portrait by Sir Henry Raeburn of Sir John Sinclair of Ulbster in the uniform of his Rothesay and Caithness Fencibles is evidence of his conviction. About the nearest that recent military costume has achieved to the genuine article are the strapped trews of mess dress of mounted and Field Officers (and as illustrated in this book by the Coronation uniform of the Lovat Scouts).

In 1881, then, the Lowland Regiments (*and* The Highland Light Infantry, to their subsequent frustration) were stuck with thick, clumsy tartan trousers, usually of a pattern they didn't want. However, gradually they adopted tartans of their own choice and in 1902 The Royal Scots changed to the pleasing Hunting Stewart. Two years later a Kilmarnock bonnet with blackcock's feather became the full dress headdress. The flat, stiffened top proved a little awkward in wind, particularly on the gusty heights of Edinburgh Castle, and a chin strap was added, first by the 2nd and later by the 1st Battalion.

The Militia and Territorial regiments affiliated to The Royal Scots for the most part wore a variation of the Line battalion's dress. The notable exception was the kilted "Dandy Ninth" raised in 1900 as a battalion of the Queen's Rifle Volunteer Brigade and who, in fact, adopted the Hunting Stewart a year before the Regular battalions.

The 8/9th Battalion, being in 1966 an amalgamation of the 7/9th and 8th Battalions, displayed aspects of both regimental and Territorial dress. The Lowland bonnet was a Territorial distinction belonging to the 8th, the Regular battalion wearing a diced glengarry. The No. 1 Dress doublet was permitted to the TA for special occasions but was already becoming obsolete. This was the apology for full dress introduced in 1947 which for Lowland regiments consisted of a utility version of their previous Highland doublet but in dark blue instead of scarlet. The other main difference was in the absence of piping around the collar, shoulder straps, front opening and skirt flaps; regimental coloured facing were gone also. However, compared to the "postmen" of English Line it didn't look too bad, although the loss of the traditional colour was regrettable. Curious, too, with the Highland regiments having their own "new look", that the Highland pattern foisted on the Lowlanders 50 or so years before should now be theirs alone to enjoy.

The thistle collar badge was still worn and a regimental badge in white metal on the waist belt plate. The sergeant illustrated wears his red sash and carries a silver-topped cane. Unlike the Regular battalion, the 8/9th wore the white spats normally associated with Highland corps and in this instance derived from the kilted 9th Battalion.

8/9th Bn · THE ROYAL SCOTS · (T·A·)
· 1966 ·

4/5th. Bn. ROYAL SCOTS FUSILIERS (TA)

BELLIGERENCE by noise is instinctive and inherent, as old as war itself and as varied as the cymbals of Babylon to the dust-bin lids of Belfast. As a martial instrument the drum has a distant ancestry of collective use to bolster courage and, hopefully, to alarm the foe. As methods of warfare became more subtle the drums became a means of communication and in this way began to serve needs both functional and metaphysical; within sub-units of an army, as in the regimental system, the agency of the drums developed a ritualistic significance over and beyond the mere discharge of duty.

There was nothing abstruse, however, about the function of the Infantry drummer in the field. The Corps of Drums was the voice of the regiment and beat the cadence of the march and relayed orders during battle. At a time when men fought standing up in dense lines and columns the massed drums in the rear would penetrate the din and direct the pace and movement of the ranks while generating an urgency and excitement calculated to stimulate the faint-hearted. As the Colours were the rallying point and tangible spirit of the regiment, so the drums were its heartbeat and, like the colours, bore its treasured emblems, honours and repute.

Understandably this solemnization of the drums was reflected by the drummers in special clothing and privileged station. Their duties required them to sound certain calls during everyday life in camp and barracks, both individually and as a mustered corps. They were highly rated for prestige value too, attracting as they did a good deal of attention upon themselves and the regiment they represented. A drummer, bedecked with favours and ribbons, was pointedly present in every recruiting party.

The establishment for a Line Regiment might be upwards of twenty drummers under the command of a Drum Major. He it was who held responsibility for the training, discipline, drill and turn-out of the Corps of Drums. Also, he was often put in charge of all Colour Party ceremonies (other than those actually on the parade ground) and was entrusted to perform services of a private nature for the officers: consequently he was always a man of unquestionable character and ability.

On the march the Drums took the lead and, alone in front of the entire column, the Drum Major must symbolise the honours, achievements and spirit of the regiment, making this apparent by his dress and bearing. Indeed, he was encouraged to behave with exaggerated pretension and was clothed in glittering ostentation. By the mid-19th century some of the wilder extravagances had been toned down, and in any case the Scottish regiments had never indulged in the more fanciful costumes. But nevertheless the Drum Major still cut a proud figure and maintained his disciplinary role being made responsible for the drill and appearance of the pipers too after the formation of Drum and Pipe Band.

The painting shows the Drum Major of the 4/5th Bn. The Royal Scots Fusiliers (TA) in 1966 in a uniform which illustrates historical references relating both to the regiment and the rank. The TA battalion had its ancestry in the Rifle Volunteers of Ayrshire who became associated with their territorially appointed Regular regiment, the Royal Scots Fusiliers, after the reforms of 1881. Formerly the 21st Royal North British Fusiliers, the regiment was raised in 1678 and was actually the sixth oldest in the British Army and became the senior Fusilier regiment. Appointed as guards to the Train of Artillery with instruction "in all things belonging to the Artillery, as gunnery, casting of hand grenadoes and fyre workes" the men were armed with the flintlock "fusil" in preference to the matchlock of the Infantry — hence the title, The Scotch Fusiliers. The fusil was also the weapon of the Grenadiers. It could be carried slung, leaving the hands free and it did not require a burning match for ignition — a prime consideration to men working with and near gunpowder. Fusiliers adopted the odd headdress of the Grenadiers, presumably initially for the same reasons (see page   ). In time the Fusilier title became a mark of status and not of function but regiments so designated were considered corps d'elites and endeavoured to live up to the honour. Prominent amongst their distinctions were always the bursting grenade emblem and the Grenadier cap in its final form of bear or racoon skin.

The Cardwell system of linked regiments did not affect those up to 25th in numerical order, but at the reforms the 1st and 2nd/21st took the new title of Royal Scots Fusiliers and, not without strong objection, were put into Highland doublets and Government tartan trousers. With these were worn the bearskin cap with grenade badge. A white plume was worn in the cap from about 1840-60 and then again from 1902. The unwanted Government tartan was altered by the addition of a blue line and this version was retained until 1948 when it was changed to Hunting Erskine. By this time the Fusilier cap was gone and only appeared on the Drum Major.

The Regular battalion of the Royal Scots Fusiliers was amalgamated with the Highland Light Infantry in January 1959 and it fell to the 4/5th Territorial battalion to perpetuate the name and uniform unchanged.

In 1966 the Drum Major was wearing an officer's bearskin cap, Lowland doublet, officer's crimson silk sash and drummers cords in "Royal" colours of red, yellow, and blue. An application for the restoration of Government tartan had been granted and it was being worn by officers and drummers, the other ranks wearing out existing Erskine stocks and the pipers being in Dress Erskine. The traditional Drum Major's belt with its richly embroidered devices and crest is a symbolical drum belt and actually carries two ornamental drum sticks.

The Highland broadsword is carried hooked up, hilt backwards, to allow free use of both hands in manipulating the staff, which is used for signalling instructions and directions to the drummers while playing. Although always remaining functional, the staff had early become highly ornate and encrusted with honours and insignia. Only a skilful and confident "Drummie" will perform the ultimate in bravura tossing and catching such a costly item.

4/5th Bn. ROYAL SCOTS FUSILIERS. (T.A.)
1966

4/5th. Bn.
THE KING'S OWN SCOTTISH BORDERERS (TA)

ONE of the problems of war has always been communication between the commander and his men, particularly on the battlefield. During the early 18th century troops were arranged for battle in a comparatively leisurely manner by drumbeat and bellowing: the opposing sides could probably see each other quite clearly and would be in little doubt about which direction to charge. As tactics developed and the manoeuvering of large masses became more complicated the traffic in orders increased between staff and units but the dense ranks of men were still controlled by word of command from individual officers and the regiment collectively by the beating of the massed Corps of Drums in the rear. In theory, by these means the soldier should have been informed and directed. In practice it was rather different; the drums gave only the most rudimentary instructions acting more emotionally than specifically and those on the flanks or rear, who could not hear the shouted words above the noise of battle, followed the direction of their officer's sword or the position of the Colours. Many of the stirring speeches attributed to brave leaders must have been lost to all but those nearest to them.

Inevitably greater deployment out-paced the existing system and bugle calls replaced the beating of drums – at the time this would seem as advanced as flag-wagging, heliograph and the field-telephone were to be in later warfare. Nevertheless, even bugles had a gradual introduction by way of Light Infantry Regiments who, skirmishing ahead of the main body in

Twenty-one

extended order, could not be controlled by drum. As the practice spread to Line regiments the bugles were given to the existing channel of communication — the drummers.

Although now redundant in battle the significance of the drums was undiminished and, as with the Colours, those things which symbolised the allegiances and achievements of the regiment were celebrated upon them. Thus the drum hoops were painted in national or regimental colours and the shell was emblazoned with emblems, honours and mottoes.

The exclusiveness of the drums was expressed, too, in the clothing of the drummers which marked them out from the Rank and File by colour and decoration. In the 18th century they are commonly supposed to have worn a "reversed coat" in the facing colour of the regiment, that is to say, where the men wore a red coat with yellow collar and cuffs the drummers would be in yellow with red collar and cuffs. It is by no means certain that all regiments followed this regulation and where evidence is lacking it would be wrong to assume that they did. Similarly, the Grenadier cap was prescribed for drummers (and Pioneers as well as the Grenadier Company) and was probably worn in most regiments until early in the 1800's.

But whatever the colour of the coat it would certainly be decorated on the back and sleeve seams, the collar, buttons, buttonholes and wings with lace in a special variation of the regimental pattern. Chevrons of lace up the sleeves were "in the option of the Colonel" as was the actual pattern. A plain white lace for the Rank and File of all regiments was ordered in 1836 and drummers' lace was standardised in 1868 with the introduction of a universal pattern showing red crowns on a white ground. By this time drummers were dressed in red, the reversed coat having been abolished in 1830. Lace continued to decorate the coat until 1939, the crown changing to a "king's" pattern after the death of Queen Victoria.

Having superseded the drum in the field and for everyday calls, the bugle was carried thereafter by drummers on duty and in fact there is no such rank as "Bugler" in Line regiments. In deference to its Light Infantry origin the cords and tassels are normally green except in regiments with a "Royal" patronage, in which case they are a mixture of red, yellow and blue. The elaborately plaited dress cords began to be worn early in this century; looped under the right arm and fastened across the chest, they are purely for decoration; the bugle is not connected to them at all and hangs from a separate single cord with tasselled ends. The arrangement of the dress cords varies from unit to unit and from time to time, nor is there really any hard and fast rule as to colour.

The illustration shows a Drummer of the 4/5th Bn. The King's Own Scottish Borderers (TA) in the No. 1 Dress uniform of 1966. The "fly" plaid is an interesting feature worn with tartan trousers since it is essentially a traditional part of the Highlander's costume. When worn with the kilt it represents the upper half of the belted plaid, the *breacan-feile*, before its separation into two garments (see page   ). The issue is confused by the military use of the term "belted plaid" for the "fly". Described by the late Major Mackay Scobie as a "miserable scrap of tartan" it was issued to the Highland regiments in the early 1800's and worn in Full Dress for the next hundred years. It was secured to the shoulder strap by a loop or rosette and hung behind the right arm, being caught up and fastened round the waist below the doublet with tapes. An officers' (and sometimes senior NCO's pattern) had a fringed edge and was pulled through the shoulder strap and allowed to hang down in front, often being fastened with a brooch. This was the pattern worn by the KOSB drummers and is the one which ought to be shown in the painting. There is sound historical basis for the use of the plaid with trews but normally one would expect this to be a full plaid worn around the body. The union of fly plaid and trousers in this instance is unusual, but nevertheless attractive, in an otherwise orthodox uniform.

The Leslie tartan was authorised for the KOSB in 1898 and although officers adopted it at once the universal tartan of the rank and file was not replaced until 1904.

Twenty-two

4/5th Bn · KING'S OWN SCOTTISH BORDERERS · (T.A.)
· 1966 ·

Historically, green was the correct "Rifle" colour. During the American Revolution troops specially trained for skirmishing and sharpshooting, armed with rifled firearms, had proved valuable to the particular needs of the campaign. The first of these units were foreign mercenaries, Chasseurs and German Jagers dressed in the green traditionally associated with central European hunters. When it was decided to train Regular British troops in this unorthodox warfare the green cloth was retained, but interestingly, more for reasons of prestige than camouflage. The effective combination of inconspicuous clothing and a superior weapon only received limited recognition then; it was still considered "unfair" to lie down and fight from a concealed position – immense battles like Waterloo and the Alma were still to be fought and about 90 years were to pass before smokeless powder and an artful foe taught new lessons.

The British riflemen of the early 1800's based their uniform therefore upon its European originator and with influences derived directly from the popular Light Cavalry and Hussars – an indication perhaps of how they saw themselves – dashing, fleet and versatile. This air of a dismounted horseman was most apparent in the officers who wore cavalry pattern pouch belts, tasselled Hessian boots and Hussar sashes. As the century progressed considerable simplification occurred and the uniform settled into the dark garb with black facings, dull buttons and badges and black leather equipment which characterised the Rifleman. Working as they did in extended and scattered formations, orders could not easily be given by voice or drumbeat so bugles replaced the drums and whistles were carried by officers and sergeants. Anything which hindered movement and the use of cover was discarded and along with the drums away went the Infantry sergeant's pike and also the Colours.

These then were some of the traditions and customs which the Cameronians inherited by adoption in 1881. Coincidently, the sombre clothes were singularly appropriate for a separate reason, too, for the Scottish Rifles were resolved to maintain the unbroken religious background of the original Cameronian Regiment named after "The Lion of the Covenant", Richard Cameron.

When the issue of a new Ceremonial No. 1 Dress was authorised in 1947 the Cameronians actually came off rather well compared with the other Scottish regiments. Rifles at least got their old colour of tunic restored to them and their inclination to simplicity was in harmony with the economic dictates of the day. The biggest difference was the substitution of the shako for a dark green Balmoral bonnet worn at first with the regimental badge and later with a hackle of black feathers.

The Territorial element of the Cameronians has its history in the Lanarkshire Rifle Volunteers who were the progenitors of the 5th, 6th, 7th and 8th Cameronians (TA). The 5th and 8th by intricate process became Artillery while the 6th and 7th were amalgamated in 1950.

The ceremonial No. 1 Dress was available to the Territorial Army for special occasions and is shown here as worn by a Lieutenant of the 6/7th in 1966. The headdress was the bonnet with ribbon tails and black feathers. The dark green tunic was, in the devious terminology of military tailoring, in Rifle colour, cut in the Highland fashion now known as "Lowland Brigade pattern". The black patent leather belt and pouch perpetuates the old dismounted cavalry tradition and was a microcosm of "Rifle" history with the whistle on three silver chains and the "stars" to which it was attached, being composed of rays bearing the Battle Honours normally displayed on the Colours. In the centre was the regimental badge incorporating the Mullet of the Douglases and the Light Infantry stringed bugle horn of the 90th Foot. This emblem was repeated in the silver collar badges and the sword belt plate. Unlike other Scottish regiments the Cameronians' swords were carried on a waist belt; the sword hilt was of Rifle pattern with a black leather sword knot. Gloves and shoes were black and the trousers of Douglas tartan.

The Regular battalion of the Cameronians disbanded in May, 1968 but the name of the regiment survives in Company strength in each of the 1st and 2nd Battalions of the 52nd Lowland Volunteers.

6/7th. Bn.
THE CAMERONIANS
(SCOTTISH RIFLES)(TA)

IN the great Cardwell Reforms of 1881 the 26th Cameronian Regiment and the 90th Perthshire Light Infantry were linked to become the 1st and 2nd Battalions of a new regiment called, at first, The Scotch Rifles Cameronians. This rather odd title was altered, and then again, finally to be settled as The Cameronians (Scottish Rifles). Although by this time the separate functions of picked specialist troops such as Grenadiers, Fusiliers and the like were rather more academic than actual, the implied superiority was frequently met by the high standards set for themselves by the very regiments so distinguished. Rifle regiments were still regarded as Corps d'Elites and as Scotland had previously been without one it was something of an honour to be chosen to make good the deficiency. Both the 26th and the 90th had better than average records for marksmanship and skill-at-arms; also, although the connection may be entirely innocent, the 90th had been the regiment in which Sir Garnet Wolseley, Cardwell's chief adviser, had served in the Crimea and India.

Unrelated, the two old regiments had worn red coats, of course, but for their new united role something rather different was devised. The trousers were of Government tartan and the spiked helmet and Highland doublet were of the style approved for Lowland units in outline, but being dark green had the curious effect of a nursery painting-book inaccurately coloured. Later, with the introduction of a shako and Douglas tartan, the uniform was much improved without losing the essential distinctions.

Twenty-five

Historically, green was the correct "Rifle" colour. During the American Revolution troops specially trained for skirmishing and sharpshooting, armed with rifled firearms, had proved valuable to the particular needs of the campaign. The first of these units were foreign mercenaries, Chasseurs and German Jagers dressed in the green traditionally associated with central European hunters. When it was decided to train Regular British troops in this unorthodox warfare the green cloth was retained, but interestingly, more for reasons of prestige than camouflage. The effective combination of inconspicuous clothing and a superior weapon only received limited recognition then; it was still considered "unfair" to lie down and fight from a concealed position – immense battles like Waterloo and the Alma were still to be fought and about 90 years were to pass before smokeless powder and an artful foe taught new lessons.

The British riflemen of the early 1800's based their uniform therefore upon its European originator and with influences derived directly from the popular Light Cavalry and Hussars – an indication perhaps of how they saw themselves – dashing, fleet and versatile. This air of a dismounted horseman was most apparent in the officers who wore cavalry pattern pouch belts, tasselled Hessian boots and Hussar sashes. As the century progressed considerable simplification occurred and the uniform settled into the dark garb with black facings, dull buttons and badges and black leather equipment which characterised the Rifleman. Working as they did in extended and scattered formations, orders could not easily be given by voice or drumbeat so bugles replaced the drums and whistles were carried by officers and sergeants. Anything which hindered movement and the use of cover was discarded and along with the drums away went the Infantry sergeant's pike and also the Colours.

These then were some of the traditions and customs which the Cameronians inherited by adoption in 1881. Coincidently, the sombre clothes were singularly appropriate for a separate reason, too, for the Scottish Rifles were resolved to maintain the unbroken religious background of the original Cameronian Regiment named after "The Lion of the Covenant", Richard Cameron.

When the issue of a new Ceremonial No. 1 Dress was authorised in 1947 the Cameronians actually came off rather well compared with the other Scottish regiments. Rifles at least got their old colour of tunic restored to them and their inclination to simplicity was in harmony with the economic dictates of the day. The biggest difference was the substitution of the shako for a dark green Balmoral bonnet worn at first with the regimental badge and later with a hackle of black feathers.

The Territorial element of the Cameronians has its history in the Lanarkshire Rifle Volunteers who were the progenitors of the 5th, 6th, 7th and 8th Cameronians (TA). The 5th and 8th by intricate process became Artillery while the 6th and 7th were amalgamated in 1950.

The ceremonial No. 1 Dress was available to the Territorial Army for special occasions and is shown here as worn by a Lieutenant of the 6/7th in 1966. The headdress was the bonnet with ribbon tails and black feathers. The dark green tunic was, in the devious terminology of military tailoring, in Rifle colour, cut in the Highland fashion now known as "Lowland Brigade pattern". The black patent leather belt and pouch perpetuates the old dismounted cavalry tradition and was a microcosm of "Rifle" history with the whistle on three silver chains and the "stars" to which it was attached, being composed of rays bearing the Battle Honours normally displayed on the Colours. In the centre was the regimental badge incorporating the Mullet of the Douglases and the Light Infantry stringed bugle horn of the 90th Foot. This emblem was repeated in the silver collar badges and the sword belt plate. Unlike other Scottish regiments the Cameronians' swords were carried on a waist belt; the sword hilt was of Rifle pattern with a black leather sword knot. Gloves and shoes were black and the trousers of Douglas tartan.

The Regular battalion of the Cameronians disbanded in May, 1968 but the name of the regiment survives in Company strength in each of the 1st and 2nd Battalions of the 52nd Lowland Volunteers.

6/7th Bn · THE CAMERONIANS (SCOTTISH RIFLES) (T·A·)
·1966·

6/7th. Bn.
THE BLACK WATCH (TA)

OUTSIDE of Scotland The Black Watch, the old 42nd Highlanders, must be the best known Scottish regiment and its tartan the most readily recognised and commercially exploited. Not inappropriately this tartan is officially known as the "Universal" or "Government" and with various colours added it is the basis for the majority of military tartans. But the world over it is "The Black Watch" and, with its romantically evocative name, the renowned red hackle and a distinguished record reaching beyond two centuries, the regiment popularly epitomises the Scottish Soldier of deed and legend.

The highly individual character of a Scottish regiment, like good whisky, is blended from subtle ingredients, not the least of which is the ancient music of the pipes. In the Clan, and then later in the regimental system, the piper was long regarded with special significance and even to-day his role is much more than decorative or prestigious. The piper's duties are closely related to the routine of military life and regulate the soldiers' day from Reveille to Lights Out with appropriate and traditional tunes for each occasion. The crowing "Hey Johnnie Cope" traditionally stirs up the day as "Sojer lie doon on yer wee pickle straw" plaintively ends it. In The Black Watch there is a regimental custom for the Pipes and Drums to play Reveille on the 15th of every month; the origin of this "Crimean Long Reveille" is not recorded but is the subject

Twenty-nine

of many theories. Every regiment has its own particular tunes for the Pipe Calls which announce meal times, "Half Hour Dress", "Fall in for Parade" and so forth. In some, when the defaulters are marched before the commanding officer, the duty piper adds wry comment and sparse comfort with "A man's a man for a' that".

Curiously, in the late 18th and early 19th centuries when Scottish soldiers, inspired in war by their music, were creating a legend the War Office refused to acknowledge the pipes. But while authority bleakly ignored, or worse, tried to abolish, the "barbaric instruments" the Scottish regiments more resolutely kept them. Pipers were hidden on Inspection Day and craftily entered in the muster roll as "Fifers" or "Drummers" so that they might enjoy the privilege of extra duty pay. At this time they were distributed one or two to each company of the battalion and played independently according to the activities of the men. Official recognition came at last in 1854 and then only for some Highland regiments — for Lowlanders the opposition remained. In any case the permitted establishment of a Pipe Major and five pipers was regarded as pretty niggardly and was frequently augmented, particularly in view of an innovation which was to be far reaching and permanent.

During the 1850's it became fashionable for the drums and company pipers to play together in unison as a band. Although all the pipers had combined on *some* occasions previously (the pipes of the 71st Highland Light Infantry played together in the centre of the column on the road to Waterloo) this effective partnership with the corps of drums was something rather new and different which was very soon applied to the parade ground and to ceremonial. Perhaps it was this slight shift of status and the, albeit pale, glow of official recognition which hastened the change in the pipers' appearance. At first they had been clothed similarly to the Rank and File with feather bonnet and red coat. Gradually distinctions evolved, usually in the retention of traditional items discontinued for the men — principally these were the broadsword and dirk on their black leather belts and the wearing of the full plaid. Other variations such as "wings" or an officer's style of coat were to be seen, as was the introduction of a different tartan. In The Black Watch for instance, the pipers appear to have adopted a red-based tartan for the kilt and plaid from a fairly early date although the pipe-bag probably remained of regimental tartan or plain green. Eventually Royal Stewart was sanctioned for the Black Watch pipers and from 1840-56 a coatee of Regimental tartan was worn.

However, in the 1850's a lasting change occurred in the dress of Highland military pipers when the colour of the jacket was altered to a dark green. The 79th Cameron Highlanders were first to do this, probably because green was their facings' colour. Other regiments copied the style and the green doublet has remained to this day as the universally acceptable pipers' garb with blue a close second — red is now never seen for military pipers. About the same time a new headdress, the Glengarry, was introduced for pipers; The Black Watch were affected by this in that they were the only exception and retained the feather bonnet, as indeed they still do.

Also unique is the famous and immediately recognisable red hackle which is so proudly displayed on all forms of headdress, even, at one time, on the steel helmet. The red feathers were issued on a parade in June, 1795 probably at Royston in Hertfordshire. A popular legend connected this distinction with an action fought by the 42nd in Flanders and was supposed to mark and commemorate its conduct where another regiment failed. Contemporary support of this is conspicuously absent and it is much more likely that the custom was one which evolved during the long service in North America and was ultimately sanctioned in the light of the regiment's behaviour in the Flanders campaign. What is unusual, however, was the exclusive use of one colour to a particular regiment, a right and a privilege which was clearly conferred solely upon The Black Watch by an Army Order of 1822.

The figure opposite illustrates the uniform of a piper of the 6/7th Bn. The Black Watch (TA) in 1966. He wears the Highland No. 1 Dress jacket, Royal Stewart tartan with hair sporran, the feather bonnet and buckled shoes with dress hose.

6/7th Bn · THE BLACK WATCH · (T·A·)
· 1966 ·

5/6th. Bn. THE HIGHLAND LIGHT INFANTRY (TA)

THE Regular battalion of the Highland Light Infantry (The City of Glasgow Regiment) was erased from the Army List on amalgamation with the Royal Scots Fusiliers in 1959, a shot-gun union which both parties vigorously resisted; not, it must be said, through animosity for each other but in protest against the many ill-considered aspects of the marriage. Happily the offspring, the Royal Highland Fusiliers, very quickly became a regiment in which old HLI and RSF men would have cause for pride. At the time too, there was a crumb of comfort for those citizens of Glasgow who mourned for their lost regiment (and over 100,000 had demonstrated their support of it in a mass rally in George Square) in that the name still survived in the Territorial Army and the 5/6th Bn. The Highland Light Infantry (TA).

Not only the name but the uniforms and insignia of the Regular battalion continued in the Territorials with only small differences. Historically the Highland Light Infantry had always been somewhat unorthodox in the matter of dress; in any case the Scottish regiments collectively with their contradictory blend of the national, functional and traditional were the continual despair of successive Clothing Boards but none more so perhaps than the old 71st HLI. They, for almost a century, achieved the improbable combination of Highland *and* Light Infantry costume, a story which cannot be told here in detail although a little should be said about the significance of the kilt and a popular misconception provoked by the loss of it.

In the beginning the regiment wore full Highland dress of feathered bonnet, kilt and plaid, and apart from contingencies of service continued so to do until 1809 when they were chosen for training as one of the new Light Infantry corps. High as this honour might be, the regiment deplored the loss of Highland status and after representations this was retained along with the diced bonnet shaped as a shako. The adoption of trousers to comply with their new role probably mattered rather less, for the kilt was not then regarded with too much romantic importance and, in fact, was hardly ever worn by officers either on or off parade.

By the time of the tartan revival of the 1820's and 30's the 71st were quite well satisfied with their distinctive bonnet/shako and, eventually, tartan trousers. What they could not forsee was that in the Army Reforms of 1881 Lowland Scottish regiments were going to opt for a very similar costume and the HLI would, by association, be considered one of them. By the turn of the century the position had become invidious, with the HLI fiercely asserting their rightful status while some Lowlanders, and not a few Highlanders, thought they were being presumptuous. Requests for the return of the kilt were met with evasions and refusals until at last, in 1947, official recognition of Highland status and an issue of the kilt was granted.

Very shortly afterwards a new ceremonial dress was devised for the Army but to the regret of traditionalists the scarlet of the British "red coat" had all but disappeared except for the Household troops and some bandsmen. The only place it survived among the Line and TA was in officers' Mess Dress.

A special form of dress for wearing in Mess was first authorised early in the 1870's and received official blessing in the published Dress Regulations of 1874. This was a clear case of authority acknowledging what was already an established custom — a recurring situation which has always accounted for a substantial proportion of the changes in military fashion. Dress Regulations of 1846 had stated sternly that "Officers are to continue as heretofore to wear their Dress uniform at Mess", leaving in no doubt those regiments who had been agitating to adopt something more comfortable for dining than the thick, tight, laced coatee.

A custom of wearing the short drill shell-jacket, open with a waistcoat, had been brought back from India and was beginning to spread at home. A sharp rebuke from the C-in-C made little difference and by the 1860's most regiments had copied the idea. Authority finally gave in, and in 1874 prescribed a standard pattern of shell for Mess. It was to be edged with gold braid, have a row of studs down the front and would be worn open but with the stand-up collar hooked. The waistcoat advised for Highland regiments was to be "as for Line, or of Regimental Tartan". The 71st wore a white waistcoat but in the matter of the jacket apparently saw no reason for change and continued to wear the same as before; this was the scarlet drill jacket with buff-coloured collar and gauntlet-shaped cuffs. On duty it was worn completely closed, of course, but in Mess it was left unbuttoned and the collar was turned down flat, causing the front to form rolled lapels which displayed the quilted cherry silk lining. The only concession was to exchange the heavy, trefoil-ended gold shoulder cords for plain double-twist cords.

After the Army Reforms of 1881 and consequent changes in dress the 71st (now the 1st Bn. The Highland Light Infantry), complied with the regulations and adopted the standard jacket and a Mackenzie tartan waistcoat edged with gold braid. Characteristically, the collar of the jacket was worn flat as before. But in 1895 they went back again to the old pattern and retained this thereafter unchanged — apart from a short time in the 1920's when a universally disliked mess coatee was introduced for everybody in the interests of economy.

Prior to the return of the kilt the mess jacket was worn with tight fitting strapped trews and short mess "wellingtons". With the kilt the hair sporran reappeared and full hose worn with buckled shoes. The illustration shows a Major of the 5/6th Bn. The Highland Light Infantry (TA) in 1966 wearing this exceedingly elegant dress. The jacket still retains all the features of the old drill shell; the quilted lining remains and the cuff still carries four small buttons in a fly on the rear seam; edges are still piped in white. It is interesting, too, that long after the jacket ceased to double for Mess and Drill many continued to be tailored with a full set of ten buttons on the front although only four show below the lapel. By this time the "correct" shoulder cords have been replaced. Apart from the rosettes on the kilt, an old 6th HLI custom, the dress is identical to that of the Regular 1st Bn. before the amalgamation.

5/6th Bn · HIGHLAND LIGHT INFANTRY · (T·A·)
·1966·

11th. Bn. SEAFORTH HIGHLANDERS (TA)

WHEN the Territorial Army was reconstituted in 1947 the Seaforth regimental area was represented by the 11th Bn. Seaforth Highlanders (TA). The uniform was that of the Regular battalion and is illustrated here by an officer in the No. 1 Dress which was available to the Territorial battalion up until 1964 if required. In it are to be found elements of the dress and traditions of the 1st and 2nd Bns. of the Seaforth Highlanders as formed in 1881 by the linking of the 72nd and 78th Highlanders respectively. Since both of these regiments shared a common ancestry in the Mackenzie family of Seaforth this had been an agreeable union to them.

Rather confusingly, the 72nd had been raised in 1778 as the 78th Seaforth Highlanders and was later renumbered the 72nd. It was one of the five kilted regiments to be removed from the Highland establishment in 1809 due to recruiting difficulties and clothed as English Line. The 78th (Ross-shire Buffs) was raised in 1793 and soon achieved honour and distinction in India. Throughout its existence the 78th wore Mackenzie tartan; meanwhile the 72nd was restored to Highland status in 1823 with the title of "Duke of Albany's Own" and a return to national dress in trews of Prince Charles Stewart tartan and the feathered bonnet.

The Seaforth Highlanders and The Queen's Own Cameron Highlanders amalgamated amicably in 1961 so that latterly it was only in the Territorial battalion that the old Seaforth traditions could be seen unchanged. One of these was the wearing of two badges on each side of the collar, a custom dating from 1881. Nearest to the opening is the cypher "F" of Frederick, Duke of Albany surmounting a scroll bearing "Caber Feidh", these being 72nd distinctions; beside it is the Elephant commemorating the gallant conduct of the 78th at Assaye, 1803. The other insignia on bonnet, cross-belt and waist belt plates show variations of the regimental crests and mottoes, the Stag's Head and "Cuidich'n Righ" being of great antiquity as is the war cry "Tulloch Ard". The cypher "L" and coronet commemorate Leopold, a later Duke of Albany.

The regulation No. 1 Dress doublet is of the Highland pattern for officers having gold lace on the cuffs and button loops and gold shoulder cords. A relatively undistinguished garment visually, it is considerably enlivened by the sash and sword-belt worn on the shoulders in the traditional Highland manner. This custom was lost by English Line long before, leaving only Scottish regiments to continue the old and very soldierly arrangement with the handsome belt-plate displaying crests and honours. The officers' sash is of heavy ribbed crimson silk ending in a long fringe.

The Mackenzie tartan of the kilt was a military invention later given a clan appellation and was worn by both the 71st Highland Light Infantry and the 78th Highlanders. Towards the end of the 18th century the practice of introducing other colours to the Government tartan was becoming quite usual as a means of distinguishing musicians, grenadiers or whole regiments. The 73rd, Lord Macleod's Highlanders, raised in 1777, added red and buff lines to the Black Watch tartan. The Earl of Seaforth's 78th, raised the following year, added red and white lines in a similar pattern. Lord Macleod being a Mackenzie the 73rd called their tartan the "Mackenzie-Macleod" but later changed the buff lines to white making it the same as the 78th. In 1786 both regiments were renumbered, the 73rd becoming the 71st and the 78th the 72nd. But to Messrs. Wilson of Bannockburn (manufacturers of army tartan until about 1880) the red/white pattern was known as the "78th" although later, diplomatically, they called it "71st" in correspondence with that regiment until eventually it became generally accepted as "Mackenzie". The difference in the 71st and Seaforth sett (which is slightly smaller) was probably accidental, both regiments claiming that theirs was the older.

The actual material was the old "hard" tartan in which the wool was combed and tightly twisted into a strong thread. The weave was close giving an extremely durable cloth but one which was rough and uncomfortable compared with that made from "carded" wool of loosely twisted thread. This was "soft" tartan, but being less serviceable and therefore less economical than the hard tended to be worn by officers only. Colours were rather lighter than of recent times and the pattern more clearly defined. Silk threads were often introduced giving brightness to certain colours and, indeed, silk plaids were later worn by officers of Field rank or for dress occasions. In 1872 the chafing and discomfort caused by the hard tartan was mentioned to Queen Victoria and she ordered the use of soft tartan for all ranks.

A white leather purse with brass cantle was regulation for kilted regiments in No. 1 Dress. It was almost unanimously disliked, the only distinction being a small regimental badge in the centre. In the time-honoured fashion most regiments took the matter into their own hands and gradually the old pre-1939 sporrans were brought out of store at, of course, "the commanding officer's discretion". For the 11th Seaforth officers this was white hair with silver and gilt cantle and black tassels with gilt bells. Although extremely decorative and beautifully made these ornate sporrans were a far cry from the functional purse of ancient times and many traditionalists considered them an unecessary vulgarity. Certainly, the progression from a simple skin with fringed draw-strings culminated in late Victorian times, in civilian wear at least, in some monstrous exaggerations. On the whole the military managed to avoid the worst extravagances but this was probably due more to financial limitations than good taste. After 1914, however, hair sporrans were among the few regimental distinctions left and looked very well with khaki Service Dress.

The red and white knitted stockings are in the ancient tradition of the cloth hose worn by all kilted regiments up to about 1825. These were seamed at the back and held up by broad scarlet tape with a rosette at the fastening. Half hose worn with short black, grey or dark blue gaiters had been introduced for Marching Order very early in the century, the latter were changed to white about 1820. By the 1850's the long garter loops were given up and the stocking top was gradually turned down until a complete diamond was shown.

11th Bn· SEAFORTH HIGHLANDERS·(T·A·)
·1963·

3rd. Bn. THE GORDON HIGHLANDERS (TA)

We have said something of the part that the Corps of Drums and the drummers themselves played in the military scene, particularly before the introduction of the bugle. The importance of the drummer was just as significant in the Highland regiments even if at times his duties were rivalled by the pipers. Indeed, the official acceptance of the pipes in 1854 seems to coincide roughly with the marriage of the two instruments playing together as a band, and for Scottish regiments at least this circumstance gave the drums a new purpose and direction denied to the Line whose Drums and Fifes crystallised as a ceremonial set-piece.

Highland drummers, like the others, were distinguished by special clothing — the tracery of lace, shoulder "wings", Grenadier cap and, possibly, the reversed coat. Certainly there is pictorial evidence, accepted as reliable, that the 92 Gordon Highlanders' drummers were dressed in yellow coats in 1815. Fifteen years later the red coat was ordered for drummers and this, with the changes in lace already described, continued in use until 1939. It was not restored after the war but reappeared unofficially in many Regular and Territorial regiments for wear "in barracks" and made a brave show until worn out.

The drummer illustrated is of the 3rd Bn. The Gordon Highlanders (TA) and typifies the uniform worn by this rank in a Highland regiment around 1966. Very little is left to him of his predecessor's extravagant finery; the lace has shrunk to the wings alone and only the ornate cords provide additional decoration. In the Gordons these were bright yellow, as were the turn-backs of the doublet, this being the regimental facing colour. A gold drum badge is worn on the right upper arm.

Because of the position of the drum when playing no sporran is worn. The small "fly plaid" is an imitation of the ancient belted plaid and was worn by the Rank and File up to 1914 in Review Order.

Forty-one

The traditional Highland feathered bonnet, once worn by all ranks, was restored only to drummers and bandsmen after the 1914-18 war. A magnificent and dignified headdress, there has been a certain amount of argument and legend attached to its origin, arising perhaps from its early form and construction. But portraits show that a fine bonnet decorated with black or white ostrich plumes was worn by Highland Chiefs on dress occasions at least a century before the military adopted and improved it.

The soldier's bonnet of the 18th century was the "hummle" bonnet commonly worn in Scotland at the time and made of a thick cloth called "thrum". In civilian style it resembled a large flat pancake with a toorie on top and a plain coloured binding. A ribbon threaded through slits in the binding for adjusting the size possibly became stylised into the alternate coloured dicing of the military bonnet. In the Highland corps this headdress was worn "cocked", that is, shaped damp on a wooden block into a high, almost straight-sided pie with a deep border of dicing. From a cockade at the side sprang a tuft of black feathers or bearskin. This plume reached far over the top of the bonnet and eventually the outline thus formed was consolidated by attaching the feathers to a wire frame; finally they were carried right around the top of the border. Imitation feathers of worsted are known to have been used, in fact the officer commanding the 2nd Battalion of the 78th Highlanders compared them quite favourably against the real feathers of the 42nd which he bluntly described as "the worst part of their clothing and equipment". A criticism that at least credits the Black Watch with bearing the expense of the genuine article. The blue bonnet remained visible below the feathers for some time and it continued, complete with toorie, as the basis of the whole construction long after it was totally enclosed by the wire cage.

The cockade was usually of black leather for the men and silk for the officers. The normal embellishment was a regimental button, but various other devices appeared especially for the Grenadier and Light Companies. A red cockade was worn by the Light Company of the 92nd Gordon Highlanders from 1808 until 1857. At the end of the 18th century coloured feather plumes were added to the bonnet, generally being two-thirds white over one-third red for Battalion Companies and white and green respectively for Grenadier and Light Companies. The 42nd, of course, had their exclusive red hackle.

The "fox-tails" hanging on the right side were another development of the rigidly framed feathers; at first they were quite short but during the 19th century steadily descended until by the end of it they were almost at shoulder level. Regulations were for the Black Watch to have four tails, the Argyll and Sutherland Highlanders six, and the other regiments five. Behind the tails was an opening which was supposed to be kept covered by a string passed through the tails halfway down their length. But here, in the "craw's nest" the Jocks used to carry clay pipe, tobacco and items too bulky for tunic pockets but needed at short halts on the march.

Officially at least the early bonnet had no chin strap and was supposed to be worn firmly on the head, the size being adjusted by a tie at the back. This was still represented by the long ribbon tails of later patterns. A regimental order to the 92nd in 1796 directs that the men's bonnets should be adjusted to be worn properly "and not down on their heads like a night cap".

A detachable leather peak was fitted during the Peninsular and Waterloo campaigns and about this time, too, an oilskin cover was introduced. Throughout much of the 19th century rather more care often seemed to be taken in the protection of expensive headgear than of the wearers and varieties of cap covers were evolved for different climes. Admittedly the feather bonnet was susceptible to the elements but encased in oilskin it resembled an inflated sponge-bag.

The feather bonnet, perhaps as much as the tartan, has come to epitomise the Highland soldier of the last century and with its imposing height, textured, moving surface and swinging tails must be one of the most colourful and attractive of traditional headdresses.

3rd Bn. THE GORDON HIGHLANDERS. (T.A.)
· 1966 ·

4/5th. Bn.
THE QUEEN'S OWN CAMERON HIGHLANDERS (TA)

BROADLY speaking, apart from differences in facing colours, or between tricorne and mitre cap, when the 18th century opened the uniforms of the regiments of the Crown bore a marked similarity one to another, Horse *and* Foot. When it closed, of all the countless sartorial innovations, regimental and divisional, perhaps none was so striking nor to be so lasting as the emergence of tartan on the battlefields of Europe and the New World. The formation of the Black Watch in 1739 brought the kilt and plaid into the costume of the British Army profoundly influencing the appearance of all subsequent Highland corps, in time all Scottish regiments and ultimately, the national dress of the country. The dark Government tartan given to the "Watch" was to become the basis for every military tartan, with one exception, and of a few so-called "clan" tartans.

A considerable number of regiments was raised in the Highlands prior to 1800 and although all were clothed in certain items of uniform the tartan continued to be worn in the traditional manner. The general effect, therefore, while undeniably warlike was rather more civilian than military at first. The principal garment was the belted plaid. Simplicity itself, this required no stitching or tailoring consisting of a large piece of material which the wearer belted around his body above and below the waist. The part below came almost to the knees, was crossed over in front and arranged in pleats to the back and sides. The longer upper part could be wrapped around the body for protection or fastened behind one shoulder with a pin or loop leaving the arms free. Latterly the belted plaid was worn mostly as a full dress until it was given up early in the 1800's.

For working and for Undress the men were issued with the less cumbersome feili-beag or "little kilt". This was the lower part only of the big belted plaid with the pleats stitched at the top for convenience. The precise origin of it is uncertain and the subject of some controversy but it is such a logical development of the larger garment that one would suppose its invention to be spontaneous rather than calculated. A modern kilt is almost exactly similar to the feili-beag except that the pleats are tailored to lie smoothly. Straps and buckles for securing the kilt around the waist are a comparatively recent refinement for the Rank and File, the older method being to pin the overlap at the top with two large wooden-headed bodkins which were issued with the kilt.

The upper portion of the belted plaid, having been detached, it could now be worn seperately and in a variety of ways, principally as a "fly" in imitation of the belted plaid, or as a full plaid folded and worn around the body. A good deal of economy was practiced with regard to the tartan, the plaids were sometimes made into trews for Guard or Undress and the pleats of the kilt could be unpicked allowing the material to be turned four times.

The tartan mentioned above which did not conform to the Black Watch rule was the sett invented for the 79th Highlanders raised by Alan Cameron of Erracht in 1793. It was felt that neither of the appropriate tartans, the Cameron or MacDonell of Keppoch, would look well with the regulation red coat, so a happy compromise was found in a blend of the Macdonald with some red lines removed and the yellow lines of the Cameron added. According to legend the idea for the design, and the first length of actual tartan, were made by Alan Cameron's mother; recently this has been contradicted and a new theory suggests that it was perhaps in fact his grandmother.

The 79th, later The Queen's Own Cameron Highlanders, was the only one-battalion Highland regiment to escape the 1881 reforms — but not without a near miss. It was proposed to absorb the 79th into the Black Watch as a 2nd Battalion, but the royal title proved to be no empty honour and Queen Victoria herself intervened to save "my own Camerons". The regiment always had very close links with the Royal Family and successive Colonels-in-Chief had been the reigning monarch.

In 1961 the regiment amalgamated with the Seaforth Highlanders to form the Queen's Own Highlanders. The painting, however, shows a Colour Sergeant of the 4/5th Bn. The Queen's Own Cameron Highlanders (TA) in No. 1 Dress.

When a new uniform for ceremonial occasions was proposed after the war it was hoped by many that the old British red coat would reappear. Not only did this not happen but the style of uniform was altered too. In the case of the Highland regiments, it must be admitted, some effort was made to display the tartan properly and the previous doublet with "Inverness" flaps was replaced by a short coatee with squared-off tails. If the "piper green" colour was a bit disappointing at least the bonnet, tartan, stockings and white of belt and spats brightened it up so that the general opinion in the Highland Brigade was that "it might have been worse". The coat tails were decorated with turn-backs in cloth of regimental facing colour each with three buttons and for Other Ranks there was white piping on collar and cuffs. Collar badges were worn and badges of rank were in gold on the right sleeve only. The red sash was worn as before by ranks of sergeant and above.

Regiments soon got to work on "improvements" and the Camerons were permitted their unique hackle of blue feathers. It had first been introduced in 1940 following a visit to the Regular battalion by HM King George VI when his permission to wear it was requested so that, when the threatened removal of the kilt took place, "the Cameron Highlanders might be recognisable from a distance to friend and foe alike". Royal consent was granted but the War Office banned its use for, ironically, security reasons. However, in the event the Camerons need not have feared anonymity at least in the early part of the war, for they had the distinction of being the last Highland regiment to wear the kilt in action at La Bassee in 1940. The blue hackle was re-introduced in 1951.

4/5th Bn · QUEEN'S OWN CAMERON HIGHLANDERS · (T·A·)
·1963·

7th. Bn. & 8th. Bn. THE ARGYLL & SUTHERLAND HIGHLANDERS (TA)

IN 1966 in military terms "Argyll country" cut a sizeable wedge into Scotland, covering the triangle of Ballachulish to Kinross to Campbeltown. Within this area companies and platoons of the 7th and 8th Battalions The Argyll & Sutherland Highlanders (TA) were distributed. The 7th Bn. had its headquarters in Stirling Castle and the 8th Bn. at Dunoon.

The Regular parent regiment to which these battalions were affiliated had been formed in 1881 by the amalgamation of the 91st (Princess Louise's) Argyllshire Highlanders and the 93rd Sutherland Highlanders. The latter wore Highland dress throughout its history and contributed rather more to the combined uniform than the 91st.

The uniform of both Territorial battalions was identical to that of the Regulars. The illustration shows an officer in the No. 2 Dress which is now worn for almost all parades other than those connected with the actual business of making war. Introduced for precisely the opposite reason in 1902 as "Service Dress" this uniform is exactly as worn by officers in the First World War, a fact which clearly supports and illustrates James Laver's theory that the battle dress of one war becomes the ceremonial two wars hence.

The Argylls are one of the more readily recognised of Scottish regiments mainly by their uncommonly large badge and the red and white dicing in the glengarry. Unique to the regiment, this dicing appears to have been worn by the 93rd from their inception in 1799 and may have been inspired by a similar border in the bonnets of the Sutherland Fencibles disbanded in the same year (many of whose members, incidentally, joined the new regiment). The bonnet referred to in this instance was, of course, the feathered bonnet, but as fashions in headgear changed over the years the 93rd dicing was transferred to each new pattern.

In 1851 the glengarry bonnet made its official debut, being ordered as undress for kilted regiments "with the regimental band or border the same as on the feathered bonnet". At that time the glengarry was a fairly recent invention for civilian wear and was immensely popular with males of all ages and stations from schoolboys to street porters. In its early form it was much higher in front than the later versions, being really a variation of the common Highland bonnet in which the sides were flattened and the top dented fore and aft. The toorie remained, as did the ribbon tails. All manner of crests, badges, plants and feathers were used as decoration but for the military a regimental badge was worn on a black rosette. A plain glengarry was adopted by pipers for Full Dress in 1856 in place of the feathered bonnet (except in the 42nd), when official sanction grudgingly allowed, and a few years later the blackcocks' feather plume appeared. Issue of the glengarry continued to other Scottish regiments gradually and in 1874 it became the standard forage-cap for all Line regiments in the Army. For some reason uniform planners nearly always looked to the Highlands for an undress cap until the general introduction of the Field Service cap in 1902.

Those Scottish corps which marched with the BEF in August, 1914, wore their regimental glengarries and coloured stockings with khaki Service Dress and web equipment. Floppy khaki Tam-o-Shanters were soon issued to complete attempts at camouflage and after the war the glengarry was promoted to serve in ceremonial in the absence of the old Full Dress. By this time its civilian use had declined to almost virtual disappearance.

The panel of devices and ribbons worn on the officers' kilt is a relic of a method of securing the apron and corresponding smaller ribbons are sewn into the back pleats. Such ribbons were once strictly functional and only later became ornamental. Although other regiments have a similar decoration none is so elaborate as that of the Argylls; the first mention of it for the 93rd is in 1837 but it was probably worn from the beginning. For this reason no kilt pin is worn by the officers, nor, for that matter, by the other ranks. The Sutherland tartan, a slightly lighter shade of the Government, was worn by the 93rd and after 1881 by the 1st and 2nd Argyll & Sutherland Highlanders.

Another very distinctive feature is the sporran made from a badger's pelt with the animal's complete head as the front flap. An animal skin purse is not unusual in civilian Highland dress and is much nearer to the traditional article than the average fancy military sporran; in this the Argylls' badger head is rare, although interestingly, in the portraits of Francis Mackenzie in the uniform of the 78th Highlanders which he raised in 1793 he is shown wearing a fine badger head. The pattern was introduced to the 93rd by Sir Charles Gordon, who commanded from 1823–26, and was worn then by officers and sergeants as it still is today. Possibly it was originally intended only for the former but was allowed for sergeants many of whom were candidates for a commission.

Apart from minor details the Service Dress tunic is almost identical to the pattern of 1912 when an open neck replaced the loose, closed collar. Acceptance of the need for a neutral colour in the field had grown only very slowly over many decades – too many for the lives lost still wearing the "old red rag". Experiments in "drab mixture" (the War Office had a stuffy aversion to the word "Khaki") had been going on since the mid-1800's with troops on foreign service but mainly in India where khaki almost certainly originated. Mostly these trials consisted of staining white drill uniforms to an earth colour with a selection of substances variously credited from among mud, tea, coffee, curry powder, gunpowder, ink, majari and tobacco. The first home-produced drab uniforms were of grey serge and they, alongside khaki from India, saw service together in the Egyptian campaign of 1882. A standardised khaki for active service was approved four years later and, South Africa having underlined the need, it was authorised as the dress for all but ceremonial occasions in 1902.

The Sam Browne belt is now regarded pretty much as a symbol of commissioned rank but it was devised by General Sam Browne, VC, about 1860 as a practical means of carrying accoutrements in such a way as to overcome his handicap of having lost an arm.

7th & 8th Bns· ARGYLL & SUTHERLAND HIGHLANDERS · (T·A·)
·1966·

THE SCOTS TROOP OF LIFE GUARDS

ALTHOUGH Cromwell's New Model Army set an unprecedented pattern and standard it was not until the Restoration that Parliament sanctioned the financing of a permanent standing army. Previously soldiers had been found by levy, or pressure, when the need occurred and dismissed, unpaid if possible, when it was past. Now in 1660, after a spectacularly triumphant return to London, Charles II built up a small, loyal army, the elite of which were the mounted regiments of Life Guards Horse. The "Private Gentlemen" who formed the ranks of these were almost all staunch Royalists who had held the King's commission in the Civil War or served him in exile. In true Cavalier spirit the appearance of these soldiers was extravagantly colourful — a fact which delighted the populace who had grown to detest the forbidding troopers of the late Lord Protector. Indeed, one writer of the day even went so far as to deplore the swing, complaining that the Life Guards with their long hair, scents, muffs and breeches like petticoats epitomized "an age when men strive to imitate women," a sentiment repeated frequently throughout history.

Within a year of the King's return the Scottish Parliament in Edinburgh agreed that a Scottish Troop of Guards should be embodied under the command of the 1st Earl of Newburgh. The establishment was to allow for 120 men and 15 sundry other ranks and appointments; they were to be men of experience and known loyalty, preferably the sons of noblemen and gentlemen. Such discrimination is, of course, in the best tradition of a hand-picked Royal bodyguard. The troop, in fact, was a revival of an earlier Regiment of Horse Guards which had suffered heavily at Worcester ten years before. Many of the survivors of this sad affair had fled with Charles to France and now returned to his service in their own country.

Preceded by a kettle drummer and three trumpeters, all playing silver instruments, The Scots Troop of Life Guards held their first parade at Leith in April, 1661. Their prime allegiance was to the King, but since the body they guarded was several hundred miles away they were charged with other duties, specifically the protection of the Lord High Commissioner and Parliament and to assist authority against "disobedient persons."

At first these duties were peaceable enough. In 1662 we read that the Life Guards escorted the Honours to the Castle "troumpettis sounding," and on another occasion that the Commissioner was entertained by their music. But within a few years the disobedient persons clause had been invoked and they were out against the Covenanters. They rode at Rullion Green and Bothwell Brig; later, under the standard of James II, they opposed the Argyll rising and in 1688 were ordered to London in support of their unfortunate King. After his abdication they returned to Scotland and adopted the cypher of William of Orange. Some 20 years later the Scottish Life Guards were disbanded in London, most of the members being absorbed by their English counterpart.

Fifty-three

There is little pictorial evidence to show how the Scots Troop looked, and even this is very sketchy with regard to detail. However, a good description exists of the uniform and accoutrements in 1698 and this, with other material, has been used to paint a reconstruction of a Private soldier of the time.

Military costume had not yet evolved its own distinctive peculiarities and still closely resembled civilian dress with the addition of various belts and straps. By the end of the 17th century even the last vestiges of armour, the breast-plate and steel helmet, had disappeared except in a limited ceremonial capacity. In the matter of colour, however, the army was showing a preference for red and the coats of the Scots Troop of Life Guards were of scarlet cloth lined with white serge. The cut was entirely civilian, being full-skirted with wide turned-back cuffs displaying the white lining. The coat was worn open to show a blue waistcoat and breeches. The numerous buttons were of "Prince's Metal," they and the buttonholes being decorated with loops of gold lace. Prince's metal was so called after Prince Rupert; it looked like brass and was an alloy of copper and either arsenic or bismuth.

The wide-brimmed hat was edged and banded with gold lace. The sides and back were cocked variously according to fashion until eventually all three were turned up at once and the tricorne had arrived. In any form it was a hopelessly impractical headdress both militarily and climatically. A further inconvenience was the growing fashion for larger and more extravagant wigs. Natural hair, providing the owner could produce a good crop, was still seen but it was worn long, in ringlets to the front and sometimes gathered in a ribbon at the back to keep it from blowing about.

The thick cavalry boot of the period extended well up the leg with a wide, stiffened top to protect the knees from crushing in close action. The heel was stacked high and heavy rowel spurs were worn. The gloves had deep stiffened gauntlet tops.

Four personal arms were carried; a sword, a carbine and a pair of pistols. The sword was a straight-edged weapon with a lacquered brass hilt and it was suspended from a Russia leather belt covered in blue velvet bordered with gold galloon. A similar belt, only double, was worn over the left shoulder to carry a cartridge pouch and the carbine. This was a simple firearm with a flintlock action and a blued steel barrel; a bar on the left side held a loose ring to which was clipped a swivel hook on the carbine belt. Generally the carbine was held as illustrated but it would be allowed to dangle over the horse's flank when the sword was carried drawn on formal occasions. One such is described in an account of the execution of Sir Archibald Johnston of Warriston in July, 1663, when we are told "a great pairt of the Kinge's leaff Gaird on horseback with thair carabynes and naikit swordis, and trumpettouris and ketill-drum were present." In continental armies it was customary to fire the carbine from the saddle either when receiving an enemy charge or before making one. In the British Army usually only the pistols were discharged from the saddle; the sword was used in the charge and the carbine regarded more as a dismounted weapon.

The heavy flintlock pistols were carried, butts forward, in bucket holsters on either side of the pommel. Holster caps and saddle housing were of blue cloth edged with gold and displaying the crown and Royal Cypher. The plain curb bit was of the pattern known as the "Hanoverian" or "Dutch Bit" and the brow band was decorated with ribbons. These and the ribbons on the tail are what remained of an earlier proliferation of favours and furbelows which festooned both horse and rider.

By this time black seems to have become the acceptable colour for military troop horses. William III imported large numbers of heavy black horses from Holland and these were crossed with native British breeds to produce strains of powerful working animals. The Scots Life Guards was probably mounted on the sturdy Lanarkshire horse from which the Clydesdale is descended in a cross with the Flanders' stallion.

1ST SCOTS TROOP of LIFE GUARDS
· 1698 ·

2nd. SCOTS TROOP HORSE GRENADIER GUARDS

IN THE 17th century the hand grenade was revived as a fashionable weapon in Continental armies and with it developed a specialist soldier — the grenadier. Inevitably, grenadiers began to appear in this country too and in 1678 Grenadier Companies were added to the regiments of Foot. The cavalry quickly followed suit and troops of Horse Grenadiers were attached to the mounted regiments of the Sovereign's Household.

The function of the grenadier was to lead the assault upon fortfications and, hacking through obstacles with his axe, throw his grenades among the defenders. Work of this nature required considerable courage and daring, not to mention physical strength; obviously then, only the tallest and boldest were chosen for it. Very soon the grenadier acquired an aura of glamour, the paratrooper of his day perhaps, and was regarded by military and public alike as high among the elite of the army. Indeed so impressed were the military by their own creation that the name and distinctions of the grenadier were to survive as an endorsement of prestige and honour long after the weapon they served.

Although the Horse Grenadiers worked in close support of the cavalry they were regarded as mounted infantry and were clothed and equipped as a cross between Horse and Foot. Being attached to the Royal Bodyguard they enjoyed certain privileges by association but they were recruited from ordinary sources and not from among "private gentlemen".

In 1702 a grenadier troop was raised in Edinburgh; seven years later it was moved south to London for service with the Life Guards as the 2nd Troop of Horse Grenadier Guards. Throughout its existence it was to be known as the Scots Troop of Horse Grenadiers. They took part, among other events, in Marlborough's funeral procession in 1722 and were present at Dettingen in 1747.

Their appearance in the middle of the century is reasonably well recorded and has been reconstructed for the painting opposite. By 1751 there were two troops of Horse Grenadier Guards, differing from each other only in small details of dress. In many respects military costume at this time was still very close in cut and style to the civilian fashions of the day — even the excess of buttons and loops was common to both. So too was the tricorne hat. In the army it was the headdress of all ranks with only a few exceptions, notably the grenadiers, and consequently of such significance that something must be said about this.

It is supposed that because of the difficulty in slinging a fusil over the wide-brimmed hat Grenadiers, when they were first formed, were given a curious cap rather like an old-fashioned nightcap with a tassel. It was worn pendant and trimmed with fur, but soon metamorphosis began. A little flap decorated with regimental devices replaced the fur on the front, then gradually the cap grew upwards and sometimes outwards until behind the flap there rose a stiffened version of the loose bag which still often remained at the same time, visible from the back. One would suppose that the original intent was now totally defeated and that one inconvenient hat had been exchanged for another. Nevertheless, many pictures show the grenadier, missile and match in hand, balancing on his head a cap like a starched tea-cosy. Eventually fur reappeared and from it evolved the bearskin of the Foot Guards, Fusiliers and the Royal Scots Greys.

But it was the tall cloth mitre cap which epitomised the grenadier of old and it was this that the Horse Grenadiers were still wearing in 1751. For the Scots Troops it was red with blue turn-ups and decorated with embroidered insignia. The red bag and tassel still showed clearly at the back.

Natural hair was worn, heavily powdered and in the fashion usually favoured by officers, brushed back, curled above the ears and in a queue which was tucked up under the cap.

By virtue of privilege the Household troops all wore scarlet, a brick-red being the normal colour for rank and file at this time. The coat was faced with blue and the skirts were buttoned back for ease of movement. There was a profusion of buttons on the front, back, skirts and sleeves, each with a white lace loop and buttonhole. White shoulder knots hung behind the right shoulder. This double loop of cord is supposed to have derived from the rope carried by cavalrymen to bind bundles of forage. By this time, however, it was purely an embellishment or an indication of rank, being differently coloured for sergeants and corporals.

Waistcoat and breeches were of buff leather. The boots were heavy soled with a high stacked heel and a stiffened top. To protect the breeches from chafing and boot blacking, white cloth or canvas knee pieces were worn. They were tied around the knees with string fastenings at the bottom and a loop to the knee-buttons of the breeches on top. Only three inches of the knee piece was to show above the boot.

Sword and bayonet were carried on a waist belt under the coat and hanging on a broad shoulder belt was the large cartouche affected by grenadiers and dragoons. Just above this was a powder horn attached to the belt by a cord which allowed the flask to be brought forward far enough to prime the carbine. The flask cords of the 2nd Troop were red and still appear symbolically on the pouch belts of the Household Cavalry to-day.

The flintlock carbine was carried with the butt in a leather bucket and secured by a strap above the rider's knee. A little tufted plug often sealed the barrel from damp. In review order the carbine was held upright to the front with the right arm raised level with the shoulder.

The black troop horses were sturdy animals but horribly disfigured by having cropped ears and a docked tail in the current custom. Housings and holster caps were scarlet cloth with gold lace and embroidery.

In 1788 the Household Cavalry was reorganised and the picturesque Horse Grenadiers disappeared from the Army List, the men being absorbed into the Life Guards.

Fifty-eight

2ND SCOTS TROOP HORSE GRENADIERS
·1751·

EAST LOTHIAN YEOMANRY CAVALRY

THE twin conditions of international crisis and national unreadiness are a familiar pattern in British history; we are almost proud, in retrospect of how we rallied round and muddled through at the eleventh hour. Events around the turn of the 18th century brought us as close as at any time to the ultimate military confrontation — invasion. It was a race between us — and Napoleon's impending arrival on our shores. The situation was critical, for the British army was too small and too far away, but the public responded in a remarkable and unprecedented spontaneous movement to take up arms in defence of the land. Many of the independent bodies so formed were, in fact, in anticipation of the Government Act sanctioning them.

One such was the troop of volunteer cavalry which assembled at Winton Muir in March of 1797. Known as the Seton Troop, East Lothian Yeomanry Cavalry, their services were officially acknowledged in May while two further troops were being raised. All were subsequently commanded by Sir James Gardiner Baird of Saughtonhall.

In the following few years however, immediate danger seemed to have receded and a parsimonious Government moved to disband the volunteers, but obviously not without a little unease, for the Yeomanry and Cavalry were cautiously retained. The East Lothians had offered their continued service anyway so that when war was again declared they were ready at once to raise a fourth troop. By 1803 the threat of invasion was an even greater certainty and public reaction was, if anything, more energetic and determined than before. Men of all ranks and professions came forward, and excitement ran high as patriotic volunteers exercised conscientiously with unwieldy muskets and sabres, eagerly watching for the beacons that would signal the coming of the French. That year the East Lothian Yeomanry were called twice into quarters at Haddington and were assigned to march to Newcastle in the event of a landing.

What the part-time soldiers may have lacked in military expertise they made up in zeal and, sometimes, wishful impersonation. Many volunteer corps aspired to imitate the elite of the Regular Army, Riflemen and Sharpshooters abounded, and for ardent horsemen the Light Dragoon was the beau-ideal. In the previous century a number of the old Dragoon regiments had been converted into Light Cavalry. Actually, some confusion existed about the exact function of this new arm, but apparently its members were expected, if required, to skirmish on foot, charge with the bayonet or fire from the saddle, but in general they were supposed to move rapidly hither and thither. To the newly forming regiments of mounted volunteers this was a useful, varied and suitably aggressive role from every point of view. That they would be inadequately equipped properly to fill it was not anticipated.

Details of the earliest clothing of the East Lothian Yeomanry Cavalry are not known precisely but sufficient items exist to reconstruct the appearance of the regiment in the exciting years of the early 1800's. The uniform adopted was splendid and picturesque without being over ornate. At the time, of course, it was the very height of military fashion and the epitome of all that the Light Dragoon represented. On their heads the cavalrymen wore the superbly imposing "Tarleton" helmet. This splendid adornment had become a feature of Light Cavalry and was, incidentally, the only British headdress to be copied by the French. Usually it was the other way around. The Tarleton was very fashionable with the Yeomanry; for the East Lothians the black leather skull was decorated with a thistle badge on the right side and a tall red feather plume on the left. Above the brass rimmed "shade" a metal scroll carried the regimental title though much of this was hidden by the black bearskin crest. Around the base of the skull was a red plush turban with ornamental chains. Although they looked marvellous these helmets were heavy and awkward to wear, requiring careful carriage and the minimum of sudden movement; they were in fact totally inappropriate for the field of battle in almost any circumstances.

The red coat was without tails and had a high open collar. The collar was set quite low into the coat front exaggerating the length of the neck and setting off the black stock and points of the shirt collar above. A small part of the shirt frill was pulled through the open top buttons. Sleeves were tight fitting, usually with a buttoned slit at the cuff and they were set rather high into the shoulders. Any impression of narrowing the chest that this, with the deep collar, might have given was countered by the arrangement of buttons. Two rows of twenty buttons each swept out to the full width of the chest before narrowing to the waist. (In many instances this effect was achieved by bars of braid extending from shoulder to shoulder.) A third, functional, row of buttons secured the front opening. The shoulders were further accentuated by "wings" of interlinked metal chain on a blue ground edged with silver braid. The blue collar and cuffs were edged with a double line of silver braid turned into single and trefoil loops at the points and corners. White buckskin breeches and plain black boots were worn.

At this period the only weapons which could be spared were sabres and pistols. As Light Dragoons they should also have had carbines but in the heavy demand for arms only 12 were allowed per troop, these being carried by the flankmen who acted as skirmishers. The men were issued nevertheless with the large cartridge pouch and carbine belt combined. Possibly the section with the carbine swivel was eventually removed but at this stage, hopeful of an early issue of arms, it may have been retained. As it happened they had to wait for another 40 years before there was a general issue to Yeomanry of the flintlock carbines declared obsolete for the Regular Army. However, if the lack of carbines made nonsense of the Light Dragoon status at least the approved pattern of sabre was a formidable weapon and perhaps the best ever on general issue. Fortunately, the East Lothians were never to use it in anger.

A blue cloak, carried rolled over the pommel of the saddle and pistol holsters, completed what was possibly one of the most masculine and attractive uniforms ever worn by the British cavalryman, Regular or Auxiliary.

Apart from a few years of compulsory disbandment the ELYC maintained a healthy existence throughout the century and in 1888 was renamed The Lothian and Berwickshire Yeomanry. In 1908 the title was changed again to The Lothians and Border Horse. After service in both World Wars and as a unit of the Territorial Army the regiment is now represented only as a cadre of the Queen's Own Lowland Yeomanry.

THE ROYAL SCOTS GREYS

ON THE 2nd July, 1971, only seven years short of their 300th birthday, The Royal Scots Greys disappeared in amalgamation with the 3rd Carabiniers (Prince of Wales's Dragoon Guards). Without doubt the new regiment, The Royal Scots Dragoon Guards (Carabiniers and Greys) will be a fine one, for past amalgamations have shown that regimental differences are soon resolved under a common loyalty. But nevertheless the Scots Greys will be missed, for Scotland has long been proud of its only regular cavalry regiment, one of the oldest in the British Army.

The Greys had its origins in the Royal Regiment of Scots Dragoons raised at the end of the 17th century under the steely command of General Sir Thomas Dalyell of the Binns. In these early years the dragoons of "Bluidy Claverhouse" earned themselves a reputation for uncompromising brutality in their pursuit of religious and dynastic offenders. Indeed the very appearance of the troopers was sombre and forbidding. They were clothed in grey coats and breeches, black boots and an iron "pot" helmet. There is a belief that the Scots Greys were named after the colour of their clothes and not the famous horses. Certainly the homespun "gray-claith" was customary for the Scottish Army and when English red was permitted General Dalyell chose to retain plain grey. In fact the stone coloured cloth was imported from England for the Dragoons, but it is unlikely that this material — identical to the hodden-grey of the ordinary people — would invoke comment, particularly in their own country. On the other hand, by 1694 the regiment was dressed in red and mounted on grey horses for a Review in Hyde Park. They were known then as "The Scots Regiment of White Horses" or "The Grey Dragoons"; on grey horses and on English soil these would seem logical titles.

For its first overseas service the regiment was in action in the Low Countries under Marlborough. In the years that followed it was to gain distinction and honour on many fields, with succeeding generations of troopers riding and fighting over the same territories as their predecessors. The Battle Honours of the Greys testify to the conduct of the regiment in almost three centuries but it is perhaps for their part at Waterloo that they are popularly identified.

The charge of the Greys in the Union Brigade (composed of a Scots, an Irish and an English regiment) was conducted with a verve and ferocity sadly unmatched by the tactical achievement; and Sergeant Ewart's single-handed capture of the standard of the French 45th Regiment was an act which excited the admiration of the Army and public alike. In justifiable pride and recognition of their actions that day the regiment adopted the Imperial Eagle as their badge.

From roughly the same motives countless 19th century artists and engravers covered acres of canvas and paper depicting Sergeant Ewart's fight and the Union charge in highly romanticised attitudes and mostly inaccurate uniforms. The public demand was for patriotic words and pictures, unmindful that these moments of glory were achieved in spite of miserable pay and supplies, ineffective weapons and largely inept command. Favourite with the illustrators was the charge of the Gordons and Greys together – the infantrymen, although burdened with pack and heavy musket, are frequently shown bounding along beside flat-out horses and still with the breath to shout "Scotland for Ever". Eye witness accounts of this action vary between fully supporting the legend and almost denying it but clearly the two regiments mingled and advanced together for at least part of the short charge. The outcome, like the gallant conduct of the Gordons and Greys, is unquestionable.

The Scots Greys, militarily incontestable, were also visually impressive. Like their feather-bonneted, pibroch-playing countrymen in the Infantry of the Line, the Greys attracted attention wherever they served and burnished an already glittering reputation. Their appearance was commanding with the splendid heavy grey horses, the scarlet tunics and, unique in British cavalry, the glossy black bearskin cap. Only in the First World War did the grey horses vanish for a time – at first under chestnut camouflage dye and later when the regiment fought dismounted, a role close to the true function of Dragoons. And so, trenches, barbed wire and machinery ended centuries of horse-soldiering, although the Greys were privileged to remain mounted to the very limit of the era. Partly this was from Scottish affection which vociferously opposed mechanisation in 1937. Inevitably this had to come and although the regiment rode into the Second World War, by 1941 they had exchanged their horses for "ironmongery".

The probable appearance of the regiment during the 1815 Waterloo campaign is shown in the plate opposite as reconstructed from the nearest contemporary sources. The bearskin cap was quite small at this time. It was decorated with a brass plate bearing the Royal Cypher, yellow cords and the white horse of Hanover on the back of the crown. A white feather plume was normally worn on the left side but it is likely to have been removed in Marching Order. In fact the cap might have been covered by a foulweather oilskin – almost certainly these would be worn on the eve of the battle which was a night of torrential rain. The red coat was faced with yellow cotton lace on either side of the hooked front. Breeches and boots were covered by blue-grey overalls which were fastened up the sides with a row of buttons. A white buff leather double belt over the left shoulder carried the cartridge box and the carbine on a swivel clip. The sword and sabretache hung from the waist-belt which was worn over a yellow and blue girdle.

At this period heavy cavalry were equipped with an ugly cumbersome sword with a long straight blade. A powerful arm and wrist would be needed to wield such a weapon to any effect; that Sergeant Ewart despatched three opponents in almost as many minutes in violent combat is some indication of his physique and determination.

A white haversack and blue wooden water-bottle were carried below the left arm.

Saddlery was the Heavy Dragoon pattern with double bridle and picketing strap coiled at the saddle. The rolled cloak was carried in front of the saddle with the water-deck strapped over it – this was a piece of proofed canvas used to cover the equipment when it was lying on the ground. The round valise at the back contained personal clothing and grooming tackle. Feed bags were slung on either side when on the march.

Happily, the Imperial Eagle will continue as the badge of The Royal Scots Dragoon Guards (backed by the carbines of the 3rd Carabiniers) – the link with Waterloo will remain although the Greys have gone. The conduct of the regiment on that field drew comment from both great commanders; Wellington is said to have wished "Would that there were more of the Greys," and Napoleon, fascinated by their spectacular charge uttered surely the ultimate accolade, "Ces terribles chevaux gris!"

THE SCOTS GREYS
2ND ROYAL NORTH BRITISH DRAGOONS
·1815·

THE LANARKSHIRE YEOMANRY

CRADLED in the lush central lowlands of Scotland the county of Lanarkshire at the close of the 18th century was still largely an agricultural area. Drove roads from the North crossed pasturelands whose rich, heavy soil supported prosperous sheep and dairy farms. But change, when it came with the new century, was rapid and dramatic: industrialisation pushed into the country, cottage weavers were drawn into grim factories, iron foundries rose along the Clyde and coal bings reared out of the earth too fast for the human spirit to endure. Appalling working conditions, miserable homes and unrelieved poverty created a discontent which finally broke in the 1820's.

Into this atmosphere of growing unrest the Lanarkshire Yeomanry was formed, possibly in 1819. Ambiguity in the records suggests an earlier date as indeed does the alacrity with which the new regiment (presumably almost totally untrained) was employed in aid of the Civil Power. Certainly, a regiment of Lanarkshire Fencible Cavalry had existed 30 years before. It had been detailed to the south coast of England for Home Defence: there it was ordered to hand over its horses to the Light Dragoons and the men to proceed back to Glasgow by foot! This was a blatant hint to join the Regular Cavalry which must have been swallowed by a good many faced with a long tramp home through people as alien as those they had come to fight. The fencibles may account for the county's delay in joining the volunteer fever of 1803. Whatever the truth it is a fact that in the autumn of 1819 two troops of Upper Ward Yeomanry were raised at Carnwath and either Douglas or Lanark. Major Norman Lockhart commanded with a Sergeant Major of the Scots Greys as Drill Instructor.

The corps assembled for a week's Permanent Duty the following year and was immediately rebuked by the War Office for doing so — apparently enthusiasm had exceeded understanding of the regulations, for the Pay Office refused to grant allowances to a corps of less than three troops. The remedy was obvious and within another year the 3rd Lesmahagow Troop was added.

But meanwhile the regiment had already performed active duty being among the 2000 horsemen sent into Glasgow to suppress the Radical Rebellion. The insurgents, although driven by despair to attempt revolution, were quickly subdued and dispersed by the steadiness and imperturbability of the troops. In the case of the Lanarkshire Yeomen this must reflect the high character of the rank and file, for they were very new and militarily innocent. The officers, as was customary, came from all the families of distinction in the county, drawn probably as much by a spirit of adventure as of service. The ranks were recruited mainly from countrymen, small landowners, tenant farmers and some professional men. What they lacked in discipline and training was more than balanced by their good sense and responsibility and even if the attitude to drill was somewhat individualistic they were, nevertheless, gladly trusted by authority in the control of riot and disorder. Trouble had obviously been anticipated in the now densely industrialised areas of Ayrshire and Lanarkshire, for the yeomanry regiments of these counties were the only two to survive a general disbandment in Scotland in 1838.

Patterns of life and work were changing fast and in the 30 or so years of painful reform the regiment was called out variously to Carluke, Hamilton, Holytown and Coatbridge. On one occasion the Yeomen were compelled to draw swords and found, as others have done since, that the women rioter were more ferocious than the men. During the colliery strikes of 1842 the ensuing shut-down of local industry threw some 30,000 men out of work, many deeper into poverty, and thefts of root crops or stock from farms became so prevalent that the Yeomanry was obliged to mount nightly patrols. Some bloody clashes resulted as indignant country-bred horsemen pursued scampering hungry and desperate workers down rutted lanes and into fields.

Gradually, however, as the century progressed conditions improved and some of the changes altered the character of the Yeomanry too. Farms became rather less prosperous, hunting declined and railways eased dependence on the horse just enough to be evident. In the early days an essential condition of enrolment had been that every man should provide his own (or his father's or brother's) horse. Inevitably the ranks presented a rather uneven appearance, the average good working horse of about 15 hands mingling with thoroughbreds, hunters and a sprinkling of Clydesdales. The thoroughbreds looked magnificent but were a source of endless trouble; restless and excitable they were liable to bolt at the flash of a sabre. The Clydesdales on the other hand, for all their solid bulk, were quite well suited to the pace of the drill which was carried out at a walk or very slow trot with ample time for the ranks to settle between movements.

This was necessary due partly to lack of practice; the troop horses of the Regular Cavalry, for instance, quickly learned the words of command and were capable of carrying out quite complicated movements without much guidance from the rider. At times this relaxed Yeomanry pace encouraged a companionable attitude to discipline and parades were enlivened by couthy comments from the ranks. One volunteer commandant urged that the men should always observe "a ready and above all things silent obedience" and that they should learn to restrain their anger and impatience should the orders be conveyed in language less than civil or courteous. His excuse that this arose only from the anxiety of the officers to promote efficiency sounds a little thin considered against the Army Order that "commands be given with as few expletives as possible".

The uniform of the Lanarkshire Yeomanry followed the pattern for Light Dragoons. The imposing Albert Shako was retained long after it had been abandoned by the Regular Army and other Yeomanry regiments. For officers it was decorated with a cock's feathers' plume and a hair plume for the rest. The trooper who complained that he "needed a new plume, I'm jist like a picket craw" suggests that all ranks may have worn feathers in Review Order at one time. Coatees and overalls were blue, faced red, the latter with double red stripes, gold for officers. Like the Ayrshire Yeomanry the Lanarkshire was permitted to wear gold lace rather than the customary 'volunteer' silver. Swords and carbines were carried, although the Airdrie Troop was also equipped with lances for a number of years.

Additional Troops had been established at Biggar and Lanark in 1868 and after the South African War the recruiting area was extended to include Peeblesshire and Dumfriesshire. After this time too, now proved in the field, and with the formation of the Territorial Force, a new spirit of military proficiency permeated the ranks. In common with other Yeomanry the regiment has experienced many changes and reductions; at present its successors are divided between a cadre of the Queen's Own Lowland Yeomanry and a Squadron of RCT(V).

LANARKSHIRE YEOMANRY
· 1848 ·

THE FIFE LIGHT HORSE VOLUNTEERS

IN the smoking room of Dysart House, Fife, on a March evening in 1860, some gentlemen of the county delightedly conceived the notion to raise a regiment of volunteer cavalry. They were apparently inspired by a newspaper description of the Duke of Manchester's military turn-out at a recent levee, but the idea had probably been growing for some time along with the enthusiastic response to the national call for volunteers the previous year. Then, it had been the old story all over again: the Regular Army was too small to defend the country *and* campaign abroad; Europe was alarmingly disturbed and not to be trusted; clearly, unless the Royal Navy could destroy them first, there would be nobody to oppose a disciplined invader.

In May of 1859 Lords Lieutenant of counties were given the go-ahead to raise local volunteer corps and the ensuing rush of recruits astonished even the scheme's most optimistic supporters. The role of the new force was to be rather different from that of previous citizen soldiers; they were not to mirror the Regular Army but were to develop a type of warfare closer to guerilla fighting. One other aspect was of particular significance; the expenses of clothing, equipping and training the force were to be found entirely by its members. The officers and ranks, by this condition, were bound to be men of responsibility and good standing (and thereby, incidentally, conveniently leaving lesser mortals to the Militia and Regular Army).

In these circumstances then, and with the horse and the hunt being a significant part of their activities, the gentlemen of Fife were naturally eager to raise a cavalry regiment, but in keeping with the current trend they elected to become Mounted Rifles. In their early preparations there is frequent reference to the hunting field and the hope was even publicly expressed that "those who now ride foremost in the chase are ready to ride foremost in the defence of their country". Lists of names were drawn up at meets and markets, and headquarters for four troops were placed at Cupar, St. Andrews, Kirkcaldy and Dunfermline, with arrangements to share the local Rifle Corps armouries.

Most of the men were connected with farming and, the season being early enough to leave them some free time, permission was sought for immediate royal approbation. This was granted in June, 1860 and the Fife Mounted Rifle Volunteers were in business.

The Duke of Manchester's "tasteful and effective military costume" which was so admired had been based upon hunting clothes and it was decided to adopt something similar but with dark breeches instead of easily soiled white. The Earl of Rosslyn, who was to be Major Commandant, advised: "Have no pipe-clay; have nothing that will not clean with a brush". (Sound counsel from one who had commanded the 9th Lancers when they were honoured as "the very pattern of a cavalry regiment"). Accordingly the uniform and appointments were designed to be simple and practical with very little difference between officers and privates. In spite of the preference for drab and neutral colours shown by the foot volunteers the Fife Mounted Rifles chose to wear red; partly this was to echo the hunting coat and partly, perhaps unconsciously, to assert their affinity with cavalry.

At least one prospective member expressed a forceful opinion on the matter; John Carstairs of Smeaton, a veteran of the old Fife Yeomanry who was to be Troop Sergeant Major in Kirkcaldy, stated flatly: "If ye mak it grey ye'll be like a troop o' millers — I maun hae a red coat or I'll no join!" So a plain red coat it was, the only decoration being four buttons on a slashed cuff, a curious and distinctive feature. Pantaloons were blue with red piping and the headdress was a black leather helmet with a spike on top. Belts, sword slings and gloves were all of brown leather. An effort was made to reduce expense by articles already in use; the saddle was the common riding pattern and the bridle a plain hunting double-bit. The blue saddle cloth, edged red, carried a monogram designed by Lord Rosslyn's daughter, Lady Harriet St. Clair. Fittingly for the "kingdom" the heraldic Thane of Fife was adopted as the regimental badge and he appeared on the waistbelt plate and on the front of the helmet, backed by a saltire and star.

Until the introduction of a metal dragoon helmet in 1896 there were only small changes in dress and equipment: a white horsehair plume was added to the helmet, no doubt greatly enhancing the appearance in review, and a web girdle replaced the waistbelt. The regiment provided material for the tunics which were made up at the wearer's expense by a tailor in Cupar at a cost of 45s. each.

The first weapons provided were old cavalry swords and Artillery Enfield carbines. These were, literally, a sore point for years, being awkward to carry when mounted. Repeated requests for Westley Richards cavalry carbines were refused on the grounds that the Enfield was the proper weapon for Mounted Rifles. Unfortunately this insistence was unsupported by any proper directives as to drill and training. However, Colonel Anstruther Thompson and most of his officers were all old cavalrymen and therefore turned to the drill they knew. Unhappily it proved as puzzling to the recruits as it did to many regular officers who were not above tangling up whole regiments. The bogey was the complexity of the system by which the ranks must always be related to a pivot file. Colonel Thompson drew up a simplified manual and, ahead of officialdom by some years, devised a form of non-pivot drill, at the same time experimenting with the hated Enfields in an attempt to relieve the men of bruised backs and elbows.

In 1870 the regiment applied for and was granted cavalry status, by which strategy it acquired the multiple benefits of improved precedence, the coveted Westley Richards and a reduced official establishment. This last was the real triumph, for it deflected War Office threats of disbandment unless the numbers were increased. Under the new title of the Fife Light Horse Volunteers the regiment thrived; six years later it was joined by a troop of Forfar Light Horse across the Tay, and in 1883 a Perth troop was formed.

These early days of sham battles and skirmishing on the sands at St. Andrews were, in the event, untested until the South African War when the Fife and Forfars served with the Imperial Yeomanry. In 1901 another longstanding ambition was achieved when Yeomanry status was officially conferred.

In the Great War of 1914-18 the regiment served as an infantry battalion of the Black Watch — a role cheerfully accepted, although it was so close to the one it had rejected so many years before. In 1919 it was reconstituted as an Armoured Car Company and formed two regiments of the Armoured Corps during 1939-45.

During the last two decades the fortunes of the Fife and Forfar Yeomanry have been linked with the Scottish Horse. Inevitably, with changing Government attitudes, there have been difficult times but to-day the regiment lives as a small cadre and, as the Highland Yeomanry, is embodied in a Squadron of the Royal Corps of Transport with headquarters in Cupar, Fife, not too many miles from where it all began.

FIFE LIGHT HORSE VOLUNTEERS
· 1880 ·

ARTILLERY VOLUNTEERS

AMONG the tens of thousands who came forward in the two great volunteer movements of the last century there were many who were eager to choose service with the guns rather than to march with the Horse or Foot. Although these early units of artillery were all disbanded by 1811 elements of those formed some 50 years later may still be traced in our present volunteer regiments of gunners.

Between the summers of 1859 and 1860 there was an unprecedented surge of militaristic patriotism. Corps of part-time Rifle and Artillery Volunteers were forming so fast as to make the matter of seniority invidious. However, in the Order of Battle artillery corps were to rank before rifle corps and in Scotland the honour for first place is closely run between a battery in Arbroath and one in Edinburgh. In the final count the City of Edinburgh Artillery Volunteers and the Midlothian Coast Artillery Volunteers were the two most senior in Scotland, but tribute is due to the energetic Lanarkshire volunteers who mustered no fewer than 15 batteries in less than a year.

As was customary in those days volunteers paid for the privilege of membership and some for their own uniforms too. While riflemen were parading in a variety of shades all the artillery corps appear to have exercised a degree of restraint and copied the basic dark blue of the regular Royal Regiment of Artillery with only an occasional elaboration. The busby was universally adopted as the headdress with a round forage cap for undress. Gun-drill was to be taught by regular army instructors on weapons and stores provided by the Government, the men being appointed to guns near to their homes.

At this time the Royal Artillery consisted of Garrison, or dismounted artillery, and the more exciting mobile Field Artillery. At first, indeed for many years, the volunteers were regarded as Garrison Artillery only, that is to say, their guns occupied semi-permanent sites defending fixed local and coastal positions. But in the late 1880's the whole question of Home Defence came under review and the War Office decided, among other changes, to introduce an element of mobility; the Scottish rifle volunteers were to be organised into seven infantry brigades supported by a proportion of mobile artillery.

This must have delighted those amateur artillerymen who itched to get their guns moving like the regulars. In fact a number of enthusiastic volunteer corps had already operated horsed batteries in advance of authority and without the assistance of allowances or equipment. The 16th Battery of the 1st Lanarkshire had boasted four 6-pounder field guns in 1865 and 1st Inverness had two horse-drawn brass-barrelled guns; there were two Dundee Field Batteries and in 1886 the 1st Midlothian had two 40-pounder guns on travelling carriages which were drawn by horse teams borrowed from Youngers' and McEwans' breweries complete with draymen to lead them.

Probably all of these unofficial field units had relied upon local workhorses using ordinary agricultural harness. Actually this was in the best tradition of the old "Trayne of Artillerie" and which had been one reason for the establishment of a permanent Regiment of Artillery in 1716. Previously, at the start of a campaign, it had been the responsibility of the Master of Ordnance to assemble suitable cannon with skilled personnel and also to contract civilian carters and their horses. These men, who were untrained and often felt no allegiance to any but themselves, were inclined to disappear when the action quickened.

The plans of 1889 for the volunteers, however, sanctioned the formation of

12 "position batteries," as they were called, to be distributed among the Edinburgh, Midlothian, Lanarkshire, Aberdeen, Ayr, Fife, Forfar, Highland and Renfrew and Dumbarton corps. Reluctant to give away too much all at once the Government at first ordered that the guns should be drawn as before by hired horses and led by the drivers on foot. This must have been rather a disappointment to many an aspiring young horse artilleryman but quite soon permission was given to mount the drivers and part-worn regular Field Artillery harness was issued. The appointment of veterinary surgeons, farriers, wheelers, collar-makers and drivers was authorised too. In a world which still moved by horse power none of these skilled men would be hard to find, the only requirement being that drivers should not be less than 5ft. 4ins. in height and 33ins. around the chest.

The painting opposite shows a typical Driver of a Volunteer Artillery Field Battery in Marching Order of 1895. His uniform was almost identical to that of the Royal Artillery except that silver or white metal badges and buttons were worn instead of brass or gilt. Another distinctive feature was the scarlet cord Austrian knot on the cuff. The blue cloth-covered cork helmet was adopted by the Royal Artillery in 1878 and subsequently by the volunteers. Originally it had a spike on top but for men working with horses this proved to be an irritation to the animals when tightening the girths and a ball replaced it in 1881. The white canvas haversack was worn, Gunner fashion, on the right side, wooden water-bottle on the left. The breeches had a broad scarlet stripe and both boots or blue puttees appear to have been worn about this time. His cloak was carried rolled over the wallets on the saddle.

Gun teams usually consisted of six horses in pairs known as the lead, middle, and wheelers, the last being the pair next to the limber. A driver rode on each nearside horse and controlled the pair. Each detachment was commanded by an officer and sergeant who rode separately. Crew members were seated on the limber and the axle tree seats on the gun. Horses were of medium size and weight and had to be capable of pulling anywhere in the team. In the regular army they looked for a good draught "parcel vanner" with a bit of pace for artillery work. Teams of matching colour were much admired and there is no doubt that the volunteers would strive to attain similar standards.

The horse illustrated is the nearside leader, detached from the team of course, and shows the 1883 Pattern of Royal Horse and Field Artillery Harness. (Volunteers would be very unlikely to have received the newer 1892 pattern at this date.) The collar was still in use at this time and although more effective than the breast harness which succeeded it it was given up after the South African War. The reason for this was that every collar had to be carefully fitted to the individual horse which proved uneconomic in war when animal casualties were enormous — more by sickness than by enemy action. The rope and leather traces are shown hooked to the tug chains but in use would link with the following team leaving enough space to stretch at full gallop. A shoe case and the driver's canteen were attached to the saddle. The offside horses had riding saddles without stirrups and in the event of a casualty could take any place in the team with an exchange of stirrups, if need be. In the RA all drivers carried a revolver to dispatch wounded horses. The military pattern of double bridle was worn with the snaffle rein led through the back stay and throat lash.

In the background can be seen a battery of muzzle loaders limbering up during field exercises. When the Territorial Force was proposed in 1907 there was considerable reluctance to accept that part-time artillery could be of any value, a view which was totally refuted by volunteer gunners who earned respect and distinction in both great wars. Nor should be forgotten the many regiments of Yeomanry, Rifles and Infantry who were "converted" in the emergency, for they too brought fresh honours to the Gunners' proud decree — "Everywhere whither Right and Glory lead."

ARTILLERY VOLUNTEERS
·1895·

THE HIGHLAND COMPANY OF MOUNTED INFANTRY

FROM the Age of Chivalry the horseman has looked down from his greater height on the weary and often jealous foot soldiers. Over the centuries the mounted man established himself as the champion on the field and the elite among military men. By the 1800's this deification was completely accepted and gorgeous, haughty Lancers, Hussars and Dragoons epitomised the romantic notion of the cavalryman in war. To be fair, this was a misconception shared by many in the army who should have known better, and it was an attitude consciously indulged, not just between wars but even at the moment of truth – incredibly, the shattered remnants of the Light Brigade were ready to follow the obdurate Cardigan back down the valley again.

As the century advanced, however, it became apparent in a number of minor wars that the enemy had not always properly studied the manual of tactics and local commanders were often obliged to rewrite the rules in the field. For instance, in 1879 during the campaign against the Zulus, the necessity for fluid movement and rapid deployment of firepower enforced a growing awareness of the need for mounted infantry. Without further delay men who could ride were plucked from other duties, mounted, and hurriedly trained in their new role. At first, apart from an optimistic issue of one pair of spurs between two men, they wore infantry uniform only slightly adapted. Eventually, taking advice no doubt from the locally raised units of Light Horse, they were more practically clothed in a wide-awake hat, a neutral coloured norfolk jacket and breeches.

By 1884 the British Army had fully recognised the mounted infantryman and training schools were established in the great army centres at Aldershot and the Curragh. The men were drawn from selected regiments on the Home Establishment in detachments of one officer and 32 men who were trained to act either independently or as part of a full company. The Regular cavalry provided Sergeant-Farriers and instructors.

The purpose of Mounted Infantry was not to replace cavalry; the horse was to enable the man to move farther and faster on outpost and reconnoitring duties and patrols. During training rapidity in mounting and dismounting was emphasised. The men worked in sections of four, one generally acting as guard to the horses which were led under cover. Commands were by voice and bugle, the call "Horses Up" bringing the mounts to the men. In Field Firing, always practised with the horses, the sections made a 1,000 yards gallop, dismounted and ran 100 yards to fire three rounds. Six minutes was considered a fair time for this exercise and the men were expected to be first class shots.

In 1896 a Highland Company of Mounted Infantry composed of detachments drawn from The Black Watch, The Seaforth Highlanders, The Gordons and The Argylls was formed at Aldershot. While authority had clearly absorbed the tactical lessons learnt in the field, the need for serviceable, if not special, clothing was still hard to accept so close to London and the War Office. The men therefore trained in a variation of their regimental undress uniform. For some this was the scarlet serge tunic, although the detachment from the 2nd Bn. The Gordon Highlanders appear to have favoured the white drill jacket. This garment was a descendant of the 18th century waistcoat and at this time was worn only by Foot Guards and Highland regiments. History does not record why they alone were considered exempt from the injurious effects of dry pipeclay, (this being the reason for the abolition of the white coat, in the 1830's, for all other regiments). Certainly it was difficult to keep clean, it was made of a thick woollen cloth and because it was in constant use could not easily be washed. The jacket had to be regularly rubbed thoroughly with a ball of dry pipeclay, usually in a room set aside for this purpose. As it was also the walking out dress the artful Jocks devised the quick cover-up method of dipping the jacket into a bunker full of powdered clay and beating out the surplus against a barrack room wall.

With the drill jacket the mounted infantryman wore cord breeches and puttees. The latter were inspired by the Indian Army; they were still such a novelty in this country that none was available for issue and the men had to fashion them from long strips of blankets. Infantry boots without spurs were worn; headdress was the regimental glengarry bonnet; sergeants sported their distinctive red sashes and NCOs' stripes were of red cloth.

Regulation infantry weapons were carried with certain modifications to the equipment. The rifle was the Lee-Metford, ·303, the first of this pattern in the British Army. Its remarkably efficient bolt-action and magazine (the invention of James Lee, a Scottish watchmaker) survived until the introduction of a semi-automatic mechanism 70 years later. In the 1890's however, although capable of very rapid fire, the rifle was used as a single-shot weapon, the magazine being regarded only as a reserve. Cartridges were not yet issued in chargers of five so that the bandolier adopted by the MI consisted of stitched leather loops with studded flaps. Extra ammunition was carried in the wallets on the saddle. The bayonet was worn on the buff leather waist belt with brass locket clasp.

The deep bucket used by the cavalry for their short carbines was useless for the Lee-Metford and a special MI pattern had been introduced. It was a shallow leather pocket into which the butt was inserted, the rifle being held upright by the rider. The Drill Manual gave strict instructions for handling the arms in rapid dismounting but in the field the rifle sling was usually slackened and looped over the elbow. Later in the South African War, the bucket was ordered to be worn on shortened straps to prevent poor riders from leaning on the rifle, a practise which gave many animals sore backs.

In the 1870's the introduction of polo to the army in this country coincided with the increased interest in mounted infantry. Because the polo pony was held to be the ideal size for the work, sturdy, short-legged horses of between 13 and 14 hands were purchased in quantity. The hardy, well-bred MI cob was capable of carrying a man on a 60 mile round-trip patrol without becoming unduly tired; furthermore, the feed ration was smaller than for mounts of 15 hands and over.

The Highland Company of Mounted Infantry formed part of a force sent out to Matabeleland in response to unrest in the territory; they embarked at Southampton in the transport "Warwick Castle" on April 25, 1896. The detachment from The Gordon Highlanders rejoined their battalion in June of the following year, although a number of men remained behind, having volunteered for service with the Mashonoland Police Force.

HIGHLAND COMPANY of MOUNTED INFANTRY
· 1896 ·

THE AYRSHIRE (EARL OF CARRICK'S OWN) YEOMANRY

AS the 18th century drew to an uneasy close, growing fears of invasion found Britain as always ill-prepared to defend her shores. The Regular Army was inadequate for the task and responsible men saw that if the country was not to fall they must save it themselves.

In Ayrshire, in April, 1798, a group of farmers asked the Earl of Cassilis if he would command them as a Troop of Cavalry for the defence of the district of Carrick. Government approbation was granted — hardly surprisingly, for the men were assembled, clothed, armed and mounted entirely at their own expense — and by June the Carrick Troop of Yeomanry Cavalry held their first official parade. The early uniform was smart without being ostentatious. It consisted of a scarlet coat and a fur-crested Light Dragoon helmet. Each man provided his own mount and saddlery for no regulation issue was available from the Government. Throughout their history the Yeomanry, and for that matter most other volunteer soldiers, have frequently had to make do with their own resources or, at best, with issues of cast-off and obsolete equipment.

Early in the 19th century renewed hostilities with France and the certainty that Napoleon intended to invade brought volunteer recruiting to a fever pitch. The Carrick Troop was increased to accommodate the large numbers who came forward. The youngest and fittest were chosen and the Ayrshire Yeomanry Cavalry, as they were now known, were well and truly established and much admired for "the accuracy and rapidity of their wheelings, the pointedness of their formations, the bold velocity of their charge." The regiment now consisted of three Troops, the first, the Carrick, the second the Cumnock, and third, Ayr. Throughout the century the attitude of the Government, and the ungrateful public, too, it must be admitted, blew hot and cold towards the volunteers. In the see-saw of national crises regiments rose and fell in a complexity of names and dates; but the Ayrshire men were spared to soldier on, they and the Lanarkshire Yeomanry being the only two in Scotland to survive a general disbandment in 1838.

The social life of the county was quickly enriched by the glamorous cavalrymen; at balls, dinners and soirees their uniforms were much in evidence and the Yeomanry Band in great demand. There can be no doubt too, that the regiment performed its weekly drills and Permanent Duties conscientiously and with such enthusiasm that in 1817 a 2nd Cunningham and Cumnock Regiment was raised. The dress was now a blue coat embellished across the chest with bars of lace and with three rows of silver buttons. The helmet with black fur crest and white plume was an impressive and masculine headdress. Booted, spurred and armed, mounted on glossily groomed horses, these men must have presented an imposing and glittering spectacle in the grey streets of the towns or riding home through darkening country lanes.

But the history of the regiment tells us that if some were conscious of this image they were aware too of being soldiers and well prepared for the demands of duty. This the Ayrshire Yeomanry Cavalry were called upon to perform in the distasteful task of suppressing their fellow countrymen in the Radical War of 1820. Aroused by industrial changes, poverty, discontent and fear the Radicals were intent upon anarchy. Here were not merely banner-waving chanting crowds but violent, angry men armed with muskets, swords and home-made pikes, hooked like the Lochaber axe to pull down mounted men. It was these the Yeomen must face along with bricks, stones and the "cleg" – a feathered lead dart with a sharpened steel tip. In Paisley the troops endured a week of ugly demonstrations with steady discipline and humour. Other detachments of the Ayrshire Yeomanry were in action in Glasgow and in Stewarton, Mauchline and Galston in their own county.

In the years that followed the regiment was mustered in a police capacity on numerous occasions to quell industrial strife and election riots, or as escort at public executions and strike patrol. In 1848 the entire regiment stood-to for a week during the serious Bread Riots in Glasgow.

But domestic peace-keeping was back-yard manoeuvring compared with what was yet to come. Although the regiment served for the first time on foreign soil in the South African War it must have seemed in retrospect a boring, endless trek in which patience and humour were more often tried than courage. Not that this was lacking – the Ayrshire and Lanarkshire Yeomanry together formed a Company of the Scottish Battalion of the Imperial Yeomanry and these was never any shortage of volunteers to fill the ranks, even although those at home must have had a clearer picture of the mismanagement of the war than those who rode, hungry, inadequately clothed and on poor quality remounts. But these hardships were as nothing compared to the horrors of the Great War. Now the dashing horsemen found themselves dismounted, equipped and armed as infantry (but defiantly winding their puttees in the cavalry fashion) learning new skills and ways of war more terrible than any imagined. So it was too in the Second World War, horses again abandoned but this time for ever, and the regiment divided into two of Field Artillery.

In the Territorial Army of the post-war era the Yeomanry adapted themselves to an armoured role with a variety of mechanical ironmongery which they learned to manipulate with characteristic panache. These were chequered days with government scissors and paste hard at work on the Army List. Of all the Scottish Yeomanry regiments only the Ayrshire remained untouched by amalgamation until in 1969 authority, in the name of economy, claimed the tanks, reduced the ranks and would have made off with the name, badge and guidon had not the remnants stood firm. Their determination was rewarded by reconstitution as an armoured car squadron of The Queen's Own Yeomanry.

The painting opposite shows an officer of the regiment in the Full Dress of 1897. The frogged tunic was introduced in the middle of the century, being the approved style for Light Dragoons. The five bars of Hussar-type lace are characteristic but the wavy pattern and loops are a distinctive Yeomanry feature. Although silver lace was ordered for volunteer corps the Ayrshire Yeomanry were one of few permitted to retain gold.

The Hussar busby was adopted in 1893 (sealskin for the men, sable for officers) with a white feather plume. As early versions of this headdress were liable to fall off, cords were wound round both cap and wearer to prevent its complete loss; these are still seen in the gold cap lines hanging from the busby and looped over the chest.

The sword and sabretache hang from a waistbelt worn below the tunic. The sword is the three-bar hilt Light Cavalry pattern which at this time had just been discontinued for the Regular Army. The sabretache face carries the Royal crown and regimental cypher.

Saddlery consists of the regulation double bridle with snaffle-bit and an ornamental black horsehair throat-plume. The light hunting style saddle is covered by a blue saddlecloth and black lambskin, both edged with a cut-out red vandyke pattern.

AYRSHIRE YEOMANRY CAVALRY
·1897·

THE QUEEN'S OWN ROYAL GLASGOW YEOMANRY

AUGUST 14, 1849, was a day of pouring rain in Glasgow — a severe disappointment no doubt to the Town Council and inhabitants since it was also the day of the first visit to the city by a reigning monarch for over two hundred years. Queen Victoria, the Prince Consort and the Prince of Wales were to make a short tour of the city centre en route from Ireland to a Balmoral holiday. Elaborate preparations had been made including an 80-foot triumphal arch painted to look like granite. Some 40,000 people, mostly with umbrellas, lined the streets.

The day was to be one of considerable significance, too, for the Glasgow Yeomanry, for they were to occupy the prestigious front and rear of the royal procession, the carriage escort being provided by regular troops from the 2nd Dragoon Guards (The Queen's Bays). The duties assigned to the Yeomanry are rather surprising in view of the fact that the regiment was only a year formed and had begun practice drilling only two months before the Royal Visit. Presumably most of the horses were accustomed to city sounds although the cheering, particularly in Argyle Street, was tumultuous. Fortunately the pace was slow, for the procession included a number of civic bodies on foot.

The poor weather must have sorely vexed the volunteer cavalrymen turned out in brand new splendour for this most auspicious occasion. However, a contemporary observer who bravely eulogises that the heavens wept for joy also enthuses that "the Glasgow Yeomanry pranced about and did conquering work." Apparently the prancing and conquering did not escape the notice of Her Majesty and a few weeks' later the corps was informed that the Queen was graciously pleased to confer the honorary distinction of "The Queen's Own Royal Regiment" in recognition of its performance as mounted escort during the visit. This was indeed an honour, one shared by few Yeomanry regiments, and of particular pride surely to such a young force.

The previous August a meeting had been held in the city at which a number of prominent residents made official representation through the Lord Lieutenant of the County, the Duke of Hamilton, proposing the formation of a corps of Volunteer Cavalry. As we know the county to the south and east already supported its own yeomanry regiment (see page 69) as did Ayrshire, and it was probably felt that a city of such importance should do likewise.

The first few months in the life of The Glasgow and Lower Ward of Lanarkshire Yeomanry Cavalry (the title until royal recognition) were spent in recruitment, organisation and the assembly of military saddlery and equipment. Most of this material was purchased locally but the helmets were ordered from London. The uniform was to follow the pattern of Heavy Cavalry except that the coatee was to be dark blue rather than red as in the regular army. The collar, cuffs and facings of the tails were scarlet; lace, sash and epaulettes were gold; the pouch was black leather on a white belt and the sabretache was also black with a gilt monogram.

This splendid outfit was topped by an imposing helmet of a style very newly introduced into British military headdress. The 1847 Pattern or "Albert" helmet inspired by recent similar Prussian and Russian designs, was a silver or gilt metal "coal scuttle" heavily embellished with fancy scrolls and mounts and sprouting a leaf-shaped holder for the hair or feather plume. According to accounts and illustrations the Glasgow Yeomanry were adorned with this helmet several years in advance of many regular Dragoons; due, no doubt, to the fact that they were ordered and paid for privately.

The Colonel Commandant of the regiment was the Marquess of Douglas and Clydesdale and an ideal adjutant was found in Captain Thomas Paterson, resident of the city, late of the 7th Light Dragoons and a veteran of the Peninsular War and Waterloo. This admirable gentleman served actively, and presumably frequently in the saddle, until well into his seventies. It is interesting perhaps to note the public enthusiasm for the regiment, an acceptance which was 11 years in advance of the great volunteer fever which swept the country in 1859.

For the Glasgow Yeomanry the next 50 years passed much as in other similar corps — service with the Volunteers was very fashionable and the Yeomen with their mounted band were a decorative addition to civic occasions and public events. Training camps lasting eight days, generally in May, were held annually and the regiment regularly reviewed on Glasgow Green. In 1861 a realistic exercise was held on Pollok estate, cavalry being represented by detachments from the Royal Scots Greys and the Glasgow Yeomanry who made a spectacular combined charge, scattering crowds of onlookers in their path. An immense number, estimated at 200,000, had turned out to witness the battle, leaving the estate quite devastated.

There were moments of excitement too when the Yeomanry were called out as a show of force in times of industrial unrest. But as the century drew on the regiment trained and drilled diligently; sports, gala days, balls and the march to Hamilton from Blythswood Square all became annual events. In 1888 the "Queen's Own" again took a part in escorting Her Majesty during a visit to the city.

Came the South African War and the mettle of these stalwart men was tested and surely proved in the rigours of the veldt, when volunteers from the GYC formed a company of the Imperial Yeomanry. From active service with its hard lessons the Yeomen emerged with a tougher, more realistic approach to part-time soldiering. In the early 1900's khaki became the working dress and swords were put away except for a few retained for ceremonial. The colourful full dress was now worn only on special occasions and by officers for levees.

The reproduction opposite shows the full dress as it finally evolved in the previous century. The silver Dragoon helmet, now unlike the regular army pattern, still retains the elaborate crusting of gilt decorations back and front. The acanthus leaf holder supports a cock's feather plume. Coatee and strapped overalls have been replaced by tunic and breeches worn with gold pouch and waistbelt. Horse furniture includes a black lambskin shabracque and black hair throat plume.

At this time 'A' Squadron's training ground was a riding school adjacent to the North British Railway station at Hyndland, which appears in the background. 'B' Squadron trained at the Public School, Wishaw; 'C' at the Barracks, Paisley; and 'D' at a Drill Hall in Falkirk.

The regiment mobilised in 1914 and after divided fortunes and complex designations emerged from the trenches as the 18th (Glasgow Yeomanry) Bn. Highland Light Infantry, indistinguishable from other foot-sloggers save for their Yeomanry collar badges.

Reconstituted in the 20's, the regiment served in the Second World War in an anti-tank and artillery role.

QUEEN'S OWN ROYAL GLASGOW YEOMANRY
·1897·

THE SCOTTISH HORSE

ALTHOUGH it exists virtually in name only today, for over half a century the Scottish Horse was an active and picturesque part of Scotland's military family. Strangely enough, the regiment was born far from its native land and in circumstances bordering upon crisis.

In 1899 the British Army in South Africa had been given a bloody nose. The British public, who had seen it off with such enthusiasm, was shocked and dismayed. December and 'Black Week' found the country deep in despair over the disasters of Magersfontein (particularly bitter to Scotland) and Colenso. Our critics abroad were openly delighted and national prestige took a tumble. In time, public distress hardened to a resolve for greater effort and at home and throughout the Empire volunteers clamoured to be taken. In South Africa itself patriotic colonists rushed to support a host of mushrooming mounted regiments, for it was clear that the campaign would now be one of movement and horsemen would be needed urgently.

Lord Kitchener, the new Chief of Staff, was approached by the Caledonian Society of Johannesburg with an offer to raise a mounted corps of South African Scots, the regiment to be called the Scottish Horse. The choice of command was important but Kitchener knew the very man — a young captain of the Royal Horse Guards who had served notably with him in the Sudan and was now conveniently stationed in Natal. Lord Tullibardine (later the 8th Duke of Atholl) received a wire from his old commander offering him the undertaking and urging him to "send out the fiery cross." He accepted command immediately and recruiting to the Scottish Horse began, enlistment to be for six months initially at 5s per day. The ranks were very quickly filled, mainly from Natal, and by the Spring of 1901 Lord Tullibardine had easily raised a second regiment from Scots at home and in Australia. The Scottish Horse soon earned a reputation for the quality of its men, sound organisation, skill at arms and reliability in scouting and guiding during the hard campaign.

After the war the corps was disbanded and might have vanished like so many other of the 'scallywag' irregulars raised for the emergency. However, in 1903 Lord Tullibardine was appointed to raise and command two new regiments of Scottish Horse but this time, happily, on home ground. The recruiting areas were to be Argyll, Perthshire, Aberdeenshire, Banffshire and Moray with headquarters at Dunkeld in Atholl. Now the old volunteer cavalry regiments were all categorised as Imperial Yeomanry and with the experience of war behind them brought a new professionalism to part-time soldiering. The Scottish Horse, also classed as Yeomanry, was fortunate in its capable and energetic Colonel Commandant and was soon a popular Scottish corps.

In the Yeomanry the more realistic attitude to soldiering was superficially evident at least in the adoption of drab khaki as the uniform colour – gone were the dashing 'braws' of the previous century. In some regiments there was an obvious reluctance to discard individual distinctions and curious hybrid costumes appeared such as khaki tunics with coloured collars and cuffs, sometimes even bright 'lancer' plastrons. Many of those units raised specifically for the Boer War retained the slouch hat turned up at the left which had characterised the mounted troops in the war. Actually, in this form it was a smartened version of the bush hat which, on campaign, had generally been worn with the brim turned down all round and without badges or fancy puggrees and which had anyway very quickly become battered, limp and shapeless. In South Africa the hats of the Scottish Horse had been decorated with a blackcock's feather plume and this was reintroduced in Scotland at first as a working headdress and later only in ceremonial. The blue diced bonnet, traditional to Atholl and favoured by Scottish curlers, was also worn.

Although cavalry in essence, the Scottish Horse training involved much dismounted work including musketry, signalling and bridge building. Most Yeomanry regiments supported a band and the Scottish Horse, with its strong territorial affinities boasted pipers in Highland dress with Murray of Tullibardine tartan, (unrecognised by the War Office, these pipers were listed in the muster rolls as 'trumpeters'). Uniforms of 'Atholl' grey, a colour attributed to the neutral tweed worn by stalkers, featured in the Scottish Horse in some orders of dress. For instance, officers wore a grey, frogged patrol jacket at one time; eventually, in the manner of military costume, this practical shade evolved into a formalised full-dress. As late as the 1930's it appears in a uniform with pouch belt, sword and grey bush hat for levees, and was worn as well by the drummers into the 1960's.

At first the men were armed with the long Lee Enfield rifle which was regarded as a single shot weapon although the magazine held a reserve of up to ten rounds. In fact, one of the lessons of the Boer War had been that a charger or clip of cartridges was essential for rapid reloading and that unless advantage was taken of the reserve for continuous fire the weapon might as well be a breech-loader without a magazine at all. A shortened version of the Lee Enfield was approved in 1902 suitable for infantry and mounted troops alike; this was the famous SMLE, a popular and extremely serviceable weapon for more than 50 years and two great wars. However, in the early 1900's this had not yet been issued to the Scottish Horse, who consequently still wore the cartridge belt of individual rounds. A canvas haversack was carried in Marching Order with a rolled blanket or cloak on the saddle fan.

Saddlery at this time was light and practical; the bridle had a plain snaffle-bit and the saddle was the Colonial Pattern approved for mounted officers of Infantry and all ranks of Yeomanry. It supported wallets on the pommel, shoe case and feed bag on the near side and butt rifle bucket on the offside. Another lesson of the Boer War had been to lighten considerably the load carried by troop horses, who had taken the field at first carrying as much as 20 stones of man and equipment.

The rifle was normally carried in the bucket when mounted but the painting shows a sergeant of the Maxim gun detachment whose members required both hands free for assembling the gun. In the background may be seen the detachment pack-horses loaded with the gun parts and ammunition.

In 1914 the two regiments were increased with astonishing speed into a three line Brigade, nine regiments in all, and fought as infantry. Between the wars the regiment was reformed first as Scouts, then redesignated as cavalry and served from 1939-45 as Medium Artillery. Since then, in common with other Yeomanry, the Scottish Horse has suffered declining fortune, amalgamation and finally conversion to a unit of the Royal Corps of Transport (V).

SCOTTISH HORSE · IMPERIAL YEOMANRY
·1904·

THE LOVAT SCOUTS

THE inadequacies of Field Training in the British Army were tragically apparent early in the South African War when the Boers literally ran rings around the inflexibly drilled Tommies. Determination and bravery were not enough, and anyway, the soldier had it hammered into him that he "was not paid to think but to do as he was told". Forced into a more fluid campaign, the need for mobility and adaptability increased and this was partly met by the regiments of irregular cavalry raised for the emergency. In very many of these new corps the necessary resourcefulness and enthusiasm were unsparing; but quite outstanding amongst them was the regiment of scouts raised early in 1900 by Simon, Lord Lovat.

The ranks of Lovat's Scouts were filled from the pick of the stalkers, gillies, gamekeepers and hill workers from the area around Beauly and the mountains of Inverness and Ross-shire. In their role as army scouts they were professionals almost from the word go. The work required that they should be capable of operating in small, independent groups making accurate observation and be able to show initiative in quick, intelligent decisions supported by clear reports. These were diverse and demanding qualities but Lovat's men had them aplenty. Apart from every other skill they were of splendid physique — tough, open-air, keen-eyed men of the land, men in whose hands the field-glass, gunstock and bridle were second nature and whose strong legs were tireless and sure. No matter that the dry rolling veldt and heavy yellow rivers were so unlike the soft mountains and craggy burns of home; like poachers they knew the use of ground, and like 'keepers they knew where the poachers lay. Lovat's Scouts soon earned stout praise from General Hunter in whose Tenth Division they were appropriately known as "Hunter's Eyes".

That the gathering together of so many men of sterling character and competence produced a regiment uniquely talented is not surprising; that it should disperse after hostilities ended would have been wasteful and happily two new regiments were formed in 1903. These, the 1st and 2nd Lovat's Scouts, mounted on Highland garrons, were later known simply as The Lovat Scouts. The individuality of the original corps with emphasis on field-craft and observation was to be maintained thereafter in peacetime training (often in friendly rivalry with its sister regiment The Scottish Horse) and in the grim reality of the two great wars.

As scouts the regiment took precedence over other cavalry and infantry but it always put more significance upon the development of the civilian skills of stalking and markmanship than in military custom and protocol. The value of this was apparent in the First World War when, dismounted, the Scouts provided groups of specialised Corps observers and snipers. The stalker's glass was always to hand in those days, and even in 1939, when the regiment mobilised, an appeal for glasses by the commanding officer brought an immediate response from the estates and lodges of the North and West.

In terms of military costume the Lovat Scouts were born into a drab world: by 1900 scarlet and blue were restricted to the parade ground and would soon almost disappear. The absence of a traditional full dress troubled the Scouts little; being of practical outlook they considered khaki Service Dress perfectly adequate. Nevertheless, their uniform had its regimental distinctions in a blue stripe on the breeches, a three button "slashed" cuff and, of particular pride, the dark blue diced bonnet bearing the clan crest as a badge. Between the wars the men wore leather cavalry bandoliers, the inevitable spy-glass and rode with rifles slung. Singularly, the officers in Service Dress wore blue and white striped shirts with black ties and black riding boots or blue puttees, but here again, comfort and efficiency came before strict uniformity. Evidence of an imaginative if unorthodox approach to soldiering is to be seen in an intriguing photograph of 1914 showing the regimental pipers mounted on ponies with the reins connected to the stirrups. Officially there was no such thing in the British Army as a mounted Pipe Band although they are known to have existed on very rare occasions. Even the Scouts' pipers were unofficial being privately supported by the regiment. Nevertheless, a mounted piper might have been the subject of a bizarre illustration.

The uniform chosen for the painting, however, is, in itself, quite picturesque and considerably less familiar than most. Even in an area so richly idiosyncratic as that of Scottish military costume it must qualify as distinctly individual. The main figure shows the uniform worn by the officer commanding the detachment from the Lovat Scouts which took part in the procession at the Coronation of King George VI in May, 1937. Every regiment, Regular and Territorial, was represented; one officer and three senior n.c.o.'s being provided by each of the Auxiliary Cavalry.

Naturally the occasion was to be one of true British pomp and pageantry with the cameras of the world's newsreels aimed at London. Obviously it would be a best bib and tucker do — unfortunately the British Army found itself on the eve of the party with nothing to wear but its working clothes. The difficulty was that Full Dress had not been restored after the Great War except to the Household Brigade and to bandsmen. Khaki was out of the question for the big parade so a solution was found in the optional blue walking-out dress which had been permitted some time previously and which was now to be "improved" by regimental embellishments and other additions.

Out of this unimaginative compromise the Lovat Scouts actually did rather well, their basic clothing being interesting alone for the unusual combination of a blue patrol jacket with cavalry shoulder-chains worn above "overalls" of Hunting Fraser tartan. This outfit had previously been worn as an informal mess dress in the Scouts but without belts or accoutrements. Now it was worn with a cavalry pattern Sam Browne belt (the detachment wearing bandoliers), and the telescope in its leather case carried over the right shoulder. All wore the distinctive blue diced bonnet — at that time unique to the regiment. With its echoes of the ancient dress of a Highland Chieftain this uniform was not only attractive and dignified but in the uncommon marriage of national and cavalry dress fittingly symbolised the character and role of the Scouts.

The uniform was seen only on this one occasion (in fact most regiments were eager to forget their 'Coronation Blues") and therefore artistic licence has been taken here in showing a Scottish background with Scouts in Service Dress mounted and spying. The little garron pony is not strictly accurate either because the Coronation detachment actually rode borrowed London police horses and although they managed to obtain greys these bigger horses were not typical of the regiment.

In the Second World War the regiment remained a close family, being the only one permitted to recruit solely from its home ground. During and since these days the Scouts have known varied fortunes and changing roles as ski-troops, infantry and gunners; and for a time in the 1950s the beloved ponies were back as a troop of mountain artillery. Today the Lovat Scouts are represented by an infantry company of the 2/51st Highland Volunteers.

LOVAT SCOUTS
·1937·

Appendix

The table below shows the classification and designation of each of the regiments illustrated, or their descendents, as in August 1972.

Former Title	Present Title
8/9th Bn The Royal Scots (The Royal Regiment) (TA)	'A' Company (The Royal Scots) 1/52 Lowland Volunteers
4/5th Bn Royal Scots Fusiliers (TA)	'B' Company (RHF) 1/52 Lowland Volunteers
4/5th Bn The King's Own Scottish Borderers (TA)	'C' Company (KOSB) 1/52 Lowland Volunteers
6/7th Bn The Cameronians (Scottish Rifles) (TA)	'D' Company (Cameronians (Scottish Rifles)) 1/52 Lowland Volunteers
6/7th Bn The Black Watch (TA)	'B' Company (BW) 1/51 Highland Volunteers
5/6th Bn The Highland Light Infantry (TA)	'E' Company (RHF) 1/52 Lowland Volunteers
11th Bn Seaforth Highlanders (TA)	'B' Company (QOH) 2/51 Highland Volunteers
3rd Bn The Gordon Highlanders (TA)	'D' Company (Gordons) 2/51 Highland Volunteers
4/5th Bn The Queen's Own Cameron Highlanders (TA)	'C' Company (QOH) 2/51 Highland Volunteers
7th & 8th Bns The Argyll & Sutherland Highlanders (TA)	'C' 'D' & 'E' Companies (A & SH) 1/51 Highland Volunteers
1st Scots Troop of Life Guards	(Renumbered 4th Troop) Disbanded 1746
2nd Scots Troop Horse Grenadiers	Disbanded 1788
East Lothian Yeomanry Cavalry	(Now Lothian & Border Horse) Cadre of Queen's Own Lowland Yeomanry
The Scots Greys	Royal Scots Dragoon Guards (Carabiniers & Greys)
The Lanarkshire Yeomanry	Cadre of Queen's Own Lowland Yeomanry
Fife Light Horse Volunteers	(Now Fife & Forfar Yeomanry) Cadre of The Highland Yeomanry
Artillery Volunteers	102 Ulster & Scottish Lt. Air Def. Regt. RA (V) (2 Batteries) Cadre of Highland Regt. RA (T) Cadre of Lowland Regt. RA (T)
Highland Company of Mounted Infantry	Rejoined Bns. 1897
The Ayrshire Yeomanry Cavalry	'B' Squadron Queen's Own Yeomanry
Queen's Own Royal Glasgow Yeomanry	Cadre of Queen's own Lowland Yeomanry
Scottish Horse Imperial Yeomanry	(Now Scottish Horse) Cadre of The Highland Yeomanry
The Lovat Scouts	'A' Company (Lovat Scouts) 2/51 Highland Volunteers

One hundred and one

Acknowledgements

THE words and pictures which appear on these pages were not achieved without the willing and interested assistance of a great many people over quite a long time. They are too many, alas, to list in full and while all are remembered some, though they would deny it, deserve to be recorded.

Particular mention must be made of the great help given by Mr W. A. Thorburn, Keeper of the Scottish United Services Museum, and his assistant, Mr W. F. Boag. Very early at the start of the Mounted Regiments' series the magnificent Auxiliary Cavalry Room in the museum was closed through "enemy action" and all the splendid material (though miraculously undamaged) was temporarily withdrawn from public access. In spite of this frustration both Mr Thorburn and Mr Boag spared no effort to find alternative reference, to answer my questions quickly and to offer suggestions and advice from the very considerable store of their combined knowledge – always with friendliness and patience. I am most grateful to them, conscious as I am that in military research there are few short answers and the simplest of questions may need the most intricate reply requiring long research to verify.

To Lieut.-Colonel P. D. Clendenin, FSA(Scot.), I have good reason to be grateful for his continued readiness to share a lifetime of knowledge and experience and with the most agreeable of good humour. I am indebted, too, to Captain A. J. Wilson, Curator of the RHF Museum, for his help given, as it always is, generously and with a great interest in matters often unconnected with the regiments in his particular care.

Among those who gave precious time and took unlimited trouble my sincere thanks go to Mr James Allison, Captain J. Brackenridge, Major Sir John Brooke, Bt., TD., Lt.-Colonel S. A. Guild, TD., Colonel J. C. Homfray, TD., Major A. Johnston, TD., Major M. I. Leslie Melville and Major D. A. Wighton, MBE, TD.

I record with gratitude the courtesy and assistance given by the staffs of the Mitchell Library, Glasgow and the Glasgow Museums and Art Galleries.

During research for the series of Territorial Army uniforms many serving soldiers gave valuable advice and vetted preliminary sketches.

Finally, I am delighted that such an eminent soldier as Major-General Urquhart, CB, DSO, was kind enough to agree to provide a Foreword. He is a man who has been prepared to declare and defend his belief in the values of the Scottish regiment and its traditions. This book is distinguished by his contribution to it.

Douglas N. Anderson